What

"I've been privileged to know Ken McCarthy for ten years. I am a fan of his thinking and writing, and find him to be a great sounding board for ideas. I can always count on Ken to look at a problem from all angles. The over-used phrase, "out of the box thinking," really does describe how Ken's mind seems to work, so he's hard to beat if creativity is what you want.

- **Ed Niehaus**
President & CEO, Niehaus Ryan Wong, Inc.
PR agency of record for Yahoo from 1995 to 2000

"...Hotwired's been credited with popularizing many of today's commonly accepted Web advertising practices - "banner ads" and "click through rates" for example - to the business world.

I credit Ken McCarthy with introducing me to the whole notion that the Web could be a viable place for advertising. I attended a talk of his in the early summer of 1994 where he not only predicted the evolution of the Web with uncanny accuracy, but also put the Web in a larger historical context in a most unique and fascinating way."

- **Rick Boyce**
Vice President, Director of Sales
Hotwired

"If you want to know how to make money in direct marketing through the Internet, there's one name you must inscribe on your Rolodex: Ken McCarthy.

Ken and his cohorts know how to extract direct marketing profits from the Internet the way a mining company knows how to pull gold from the earth. They live by the same credo as all smart direct marketers, i.e., that advertising is salesmanship multiplied, and it's not creative unless it rings the cash register."

- Gary Bencivenga, Accountable Advertising, Inc.

According to the October 2000 issue of Target Marketing, Gary Bencivenga is the world's highest paid direct mail copywriter weighing it at $25,000 per letter advance against royalties.

"Netscape has had several opportunities to work with Ken McCarthy, including having Marc Andreessen as a keynote speaker at one of the first conferences focused on the Web as a viable business tool. We have enjoyed our relationship with Ken thoroughly."

- Rosanne Siino
Vice President, Corporate Communications
Netscape Communications Corporation

"As people who know me well can tell you, I'm not easy on vendors and I don't recommend experts, service providers, and speakers lightly. Many are called, few make the cut. Fewer still are invited back again and again.

I've been so impressed with Ken's mastery of marketing that I've included examples of his ad writing in my books and courses. His involvement in the Internet business dates back to 1993 and he has consistently given his clients (including me and dozens of my clients who I've recommended to him) straight, no nonsense advice in a field that is overrun with hype and false promises.

I know that there is a lot of interest in e-marketing. I have bought materials from, talked with, met with and checked out over 30 different "Internet Marketing Gurus" over the past year or so - and have had very lucrative offers made to me to endorse or partner with them.

I'm sticking with Ken. If you are interested in e-marketing straight talk, he's the guy you want to talk to.

My highest recommendation."

-   Dan Kennedy, author
"How to Make Millions with Your Ideas," "The Ultimate Marketing Plan Book, "The Ultimate Sales Letter Book," "How to Succeed by Breaking All the Rules,"and "The Ultimate No BS Sales Success Book."

"I connected with Ken when he was in the process of organizing a conference with Marc Andreessen on what, at the time, seemed a rather "far out" idea: commercial publishing on the World Wide Web. As far as I know, it was the first conference ever devoted exclusively to this topic and it was certainly the first one offered to the Bay Area's cutting edge digerati community.

In a region with more new media visionaries than any other place on earth, Ken has been one of the very first to grasp and articulate the significance that the World Wide Web would have on all of us."

\- **Hal Jospehson,**
President, MediaSense, Inc.
Executive Director, NewMedia INVISION Awards
Festival 1994 President, IICS, International Interactive
Communications Society

"I've known Ken McCarthy since 1985 when he was offering some very insightful and inspiring courses on educational psychology in New York City. In fact, I was so impressed by his work that I cited him along with Buckminster Fuller, Alvin Toffler, and others as a source for my book "Peak Learning" (Tarcher, 1991)

I therefore wasn't at all surprised that Ken became involved in the Internet in 1993 and dedicated himself to making it comprehensible for innovative educators and small business people.

I recently had the opportunity to avail myself of his consulting services regarding my web site. As I said to him in a follow up e-mail: "Hail Master!" I can't re-

member the last time I received such a flood of immediately useful, on
target advice from any consultant in any field. If you have an opportunity to work with him, don't hesitate."

- **Ronald Gross**, Chair, University Seminar on Innovation, COLUMBIA UNIVERSITY

"Ken's **System Club Letters** book is the most thought-provoking and inspirational marketing book I've ever read. I can see why people pay $1,000 per year to access this kind of information.

I told my entire list about your book and urged them all to read it, too. In fact, I think the chapters about jazz, your father, and Independence Day should almost be 'required' reading for everyone in business."

- **Ben Settle** Copywriter - BenSettle.com

"My POV on Ken McCarthy:
* STRONG knack as talent scout. Repeated demonstrated ability to locate specialists and gifted people who truly know their trade and are ready for the stage. This is a rare gift.
* Militant about quality: You don't put up with mediocrity in your seminars, products you sell, or anything that affects your reputation. There's a lot of old-fashioned values and goodness in what you require of yourself and people you endorse. A consistently higher standard than others are willing to tolerate.
* Hound dog for history: If I want a historical

perspective on something, I can always count on you to give me an angle I hadn't heard before. A sharp eye for repeating patterns and underlying causes.

Also a gift for stating those things clearly and succinctly. A wide lens of books and information sources that most people would never bother with.

* Clear discrimination of the difference between fads and trends. A dislike of fads but willingness to use them to your advantage. A love of seeing trends before they're apparent to others and like the talent scout thing, a knack for it. Very likely to be able to single out what's going to be a lasting phenomenon as opposed to yesterday's news.

* You're one of the best copywriters on the net. You're actually probably my #1 influence in terms of how to do specifically email. Been reading your emails for 10 years I think.

* Stability and consistency: You're steadfast in places where steadfastness is often under-valued. Creates loyalty and a sense of security in those you serve."

- **Perry Marshall**

Author of "The Ultimate Guide to Google AdWords"

The System Club Letters

57 Big Ideas
To Transform Your
Business and Your Life

By Ken McCarthy

57 Big Ideas

**To Transform Your
Business and Your Life**

Table of Contents

Copywriting

Business and Marketing Advice

Table of Contents

Beyond Business

Resources

Introduction

A brief history of Internet marketing...

In early 1994, I reached out to a young ad executive named Rick Boyce and encouraged him to take a good look at the then brand new World Wide Web.

Rick became a student and by the fall of that year he was the first person to successfully sell banner ads in significant numbers to advertisers. Thus the first Internet Gold Rush was born.

In the fall of that same year, I got together with Marc Andreessen, the co-founder of Netscape and the developer of the first web browser, and organized a conference for Bay Area business people to encourage them to explore the commercial potential of the Web. This conference was the first time a group of people ever got together to focus on the nuts and bolts of the Web as a vehicle for business.

In 1995, I organized a conference on the subject of local advertising on the Web. I encouraged attendees to consider creating local portals to provide advertising opportunities for small, locally based businesses. As far as I know, this was the first conference ever held on this subject.

When GoTo, now Overture, introduced the pay-per-click concept, I started to organize course material to show Internet entrepreneurs how to use pay-per-click not only to generate qualified traffic, but also to test online business ideas. By 2000, I was explaining this method to my students and clients around the world.

In 2002, I launched The System Seminar. This was, as far as I know, the first fully integrated Internet marketing training that covered both traffic generation, conversion, tracking and testing. One of the students from the original System Seminar, Perry Marshall, went on to become the first person to grasp the full potential of AdWords, a then brand-new advertising service offered by Google.

Through the System Seminar and the System Club, my students and clients have consistently been many months - and in some cases, many years - ahead of the Internet marketing curve.

With this book, I'm pulling back the curtain on some private communications I've had with System Club members over the years.

These letters – fifty-seven in all - cover every subject under the sun.

The purpose of these letters is to help you think like a marketer and businessperson and hopefully become a better person in the process.

Ken McCarthy
Tivoli-on-the-Hudson, New York

Internet Marketing

A Gem from the Trenches

Smart Internet marketers take lessons from everywhere, not just from what other Internet marketers are doing.

They learn from direct mail, from TV ads, from one-on-one salespeople, and from the hard-won wisdom of retailers.

Of all the people who sell for a living - and that's what we as Internet marketers do, we sell for a living - nobody has a tougher road than the retail store owner.

Imagine what the store owner has to juggle just to keep the doors open: stiff monthly rent, a small army of employees, the vagaries of the weather, the enormous costs of regular advertising and maintaining inventory... it's almost overwhelming just thinking about.

Chew on this one... and profit

In Internet marketing, we talk about 'monetization' and 'visitor value.' Imagine how much more vivid these things must be when your daily overhead is calculated in the hundreds, thousands of even tens of thousands of dollars.

The one great advantage the retailer has over the average Internet marketer is that he or she can see and talk with his customers directly. (Notice I said 'average'

Internet marketer because smart Internet marketers track their visitors and even make opportunities to talk with them directly from time to time.)

Dealing with your customers individually can be a pain, which is why so many of us go into direct marketing and not retailing, but the truth is, regular contact with customers - including customers who are dissatisfied with us - is the richest source of gold in selling.

Here's what Marshall Field (1834-1906) had to say. (He's the Chicagoan who practically invented the idea of the modern department store.)

"Those who enter, support me.

Those who come to flatter, please me.

Those who complain, teach me how I may please others so that more will come.

Only those hurt me who are displeased but do not complain.

They refuse me permission to correct my errors and thus improve my services."

Radical ideas... and ones worth chewing on.

Can You Improvise?

The ability to 'improvise' is an important - no make that <u>essential</u> - skill in the entrepreneur's bag of tricks, and yet it's a word I rarely, if ever, hear mentioned in Internet marketing circles. Too bad, because it holds the key to the whole game.

According to the dictionary, the word improvise has two meanings: 1) 'to invent, compose or recite without preparation' and 2) 'to provide from available materials.'

I don't like the first definition for reasons I'll make clear later, but...

The second definition perfectly sums up the core skill of being an entrepreneur.

The fact is, the vast majority of people need to be provided for or told exactly what to do. <u>Entrepreneurs</u>, on the other hand, have the ability to step into a chaotic and disorganized situation and find and create value with the material's they find at hand.

The world's greatest improvisers

It may be a coincidence, but in the last year I've discovered that a number of very high level marketing pros share a common characteristic: they're raging jazz fans. I'm not talking about people who just 'like' jazz. I'm talking about people who can talk for hours - or days - about the music and the musicians.

Now, I'm not recommending that to improve your marketing skills and make more money, you should become a jazz fan, but there are very valuable lessons that you can learn from the jazz world that will definitely make you a better marketer and put some serious money in your pocket.

By the way, while you may not be a jazz fan, you're definitely listening to the work of jazz musicians all the time...

Multi-track recording and the solid body guitar - the foundation of rock and roll - were invented by jazz musician Les Paul... David Bowie has been backed up on piano for over 30 years by Mike Garson, jazz musician... Pop legend Stevie Wonder, behind closed doors, is a jazz musician... Multi-Grammy winning, 'Rock Hall of Fame' member Carlos Santana names jazz great John Coltrane as his prime influence. And on it goes.

What it's all about

What makes accomplished jazz musicians - and master marketers - so amazing is their ability to create value seemingly out of thin air. Classical musicians on the other hand need to have everything spelled out for them in detail before they can make a move.

Jazz has three rules for aspiring players:

The Three Laws of Improvisation

1) Find your own voice,
2) Never play a tune the same way twice, and
3) Know the basics inside and out.

Here's how these jazz rules apply to successful entrepreneurship:

1) Be unique

Copycats don't get far in jazz. In fact, they don't exist. Unless you can figure out how to bring something <u>new</u> to the table, there's no seat for you. Business is a little more tolerant of 'knock off' artists, but in the long run the prize goes to businesses that develop a <u>unique</u> personality. The 'me too' business makes for slim pickings.

2) Think 'innovation' <u>all</u> the time

Jazz musicians are always looking for new ways to 'skin the cat.' It's practically in their job definition. Successful entrepreneurs have the same exact mindset. They're constantly asking themselves: "How can I do this better? What's next?" They don't rest on their laurels or wait for instructions. They never coast.

3) Be prepared

Contrary to the dictionary definition, improvisers are the <u>best</u> <u>prepared</u> musicians around.

The reason they can sit down and create a brand new version of an old tune at the drop of a hat is because they study harder and know more about music theory on a <u>practical</u> level than the graduates of places like Julliard and other classical music conservatories.

<u>Preparation</u> for marketers means knowing the <u>fundamentals</u> inside and out.

I've developed a test for how likely it is that someone is a master marketer or has the potential to become one. It's pretty simple: What do you read on a weekly basis? Who are your heroes, the people whose work you study over and over? What 'bibles' of marketing do you read and re-read on a regular basis?

Every serious marketer I know - and every serious jazz musician I know - can reel off the answer to these questions in an eye blink. Serious marketers know – <u>really</u> <u>know</u> - the work of people like Claude Hopkins and John Caples inside and out, just like serious jazz musicians know the work of Charlie Parker and John Coltrane.

Finally, improvisation - the ability to create something new from thin air - is <u>fun</u>. It's an adventure. Like all adventures, it can have rough and scary moments, but to me, what's <u>really</u> scary is the idea of living without improvisation.

Real Genius at Work

I'm writing this from an Internet café in Zurich, Switzerland.

Swiss watches, Swiss trains, Swiss bank accounts, Swiss chocolate. What's not to like about Switzerland?

Internet marketers have a special reason to like Switzerland. It happens to be where the World Wide Web was created. The year: 1989. The place: Geneva, Switzerland, headquarters of CERN, the European Particle Physics Laboratory.

Englishman Tim Berners-Lee, who was working as a computer scientist for CERN, wanted to make it easier for the far flung community of particle physicists to share their research with each other. Pre-Web, getting information from the Internet was an incredibly laborious affair.

Berners-Lee came up with the idea of an open, easy-to-use network tied together so that anyone on the network could easily access any document on it anywhere in the world. He designed HTML as a standardized format for creating documents, he came up with the idea of the URL, and he worked out the details of hyper text transfer protocol, the http that appears in every web address.

That's right. The entire structure of the web came from the mind of a single person, a person who chose to make his invention freely available to all. A decision which, without any exaggeration, changed the world.

I wonder how many Internet marketers know this history or know the name Tim Berners-Lee? Judging from the number of people who recognize the name Marc Andreessen, the first person to create a commercially successful graphical interface for the web, my guess is probably not more than 1 out of 100.

That's too bad. As unsentimental and tough-as-nails Dan Kennedy says, knowing the history of the industry you're in is one of prerequisites for making real money in it.

One advantage of knowing your history is it provides you with a certain amount of immunity against being snowed by the latest flash-in-the-pan Internet guru.

Today, I see the term "genius" bandied about in Internet marketing circles to the point that it's ceased to have any meaning. It seems that anyone who can give an exciting speech at a seminar qualifies regardless of how modest his track record or how limited his contribution to the state-of-the-art.

But we have had real geniuses in our medium and Berners-Lee certainly qualifies as one.

By the way, what is Tim Berners-Lee up to today?

Publicly counting his money? Crowing about how smart he is?

No. He's the head of the World Wide Web Consortium at MIT. There he fights the good fight on behalf of all of us to keep the web open and nonproprietary against companies like Microsoft that are constantly cooking up schemes to try to subvert it.

Thanks Tim. Maybe this will be the year that Internet marketers come to know your story and the spirit behind the creation of the web.

Is It Affiliate Marketing or Spam?

Affiliate marketing works - when it works - because a list owner, who has built up the trust of his list members over a period of months and years, is willing to put his or her reputation on the line on behalf of a joint venture with a partner.

It is the exact opposite of spam.

Unfortunately, somehow this basic reality has gotten twisted all out of shape.

Why gurus come and go - and how not to become one of the 'gone'

Every market is hungry for something new.

Newness generates attention... Newness generates excitement... Newness generates action.

Newness is such a powerful force that the legendary artist - and media manipulator - Andy Warhol once guaranteed that in the future everyone will get their '15 minutes of Fame.'

What he didn't talk about is what happens at 'Minute Sixteen.'

No matter what business you're in or what heights you reach, you're going to face 'Minute Sixteen.'

It's tempting during your 'Fifteen Minute Freebie' to push it. In the Internet business it's called 'Push

Send.' And that means to promote just about anything as long as there's a buck in it and it doesn't stink too bad.

I'm not going to say this doesn't work because it does - until it doesn't.

Feeding frenzies and other not-so-clever tricks

We've all seen the Internet 'feeding frenzies' where dozens of affiliates are pushed and conned into sending the same exact message within a very tight time period. It's just like spam - without the legal ramifications for the promoter, but with terrible consequences for the senders.

The marketplace responds predictably. The gullible and easily excited buy, but sensible people - the vast majority - turn their trust dial down a notch. And some turn if off altogether.

Abraham Lincoln wasn't a strategic marketer, but he could have been one when he said:

"You can fool some of the people all of the time and all of the people some of the time. But you can't fool all of the people all of the time. "

The smart use of the 'Fifteen Minutes of Fame' phenomenon is to get your foot in the door so you can demonstrate that you're worth keeping around for 'Minute Sixteen.'

As marketers, we forget this at our peril.

Getting It Right the First Time

I spent the past weekend helping Agora Publishing fine-tune its approach to teaching Internet marketing.

Agora, as you may know, is a $100 million + a year mail order publishing company. They publish dozens of newsletters on health, personal finance, investing, and recently entrepreneurship. Like all savvy information marketing companies their product line includes books, home study courses, conferences and seminars.

In the last few years, after much trial and error, Agora's made a spectacularly successful transition to Internet marketing. What was the big insight that made all the difference for them? "The Internet is a direct marketing medium."

Sound familiar? They freely admit that they didn't 'get' this until just a few years ago.

A huge challenge

One of Agora's newer divisions, Early to Rise, is devoted to helping entrepreneurs. It originally started as the company's attempt to train copywriters to fill its own voracious need for ad copy. Then it expanded into courses for the general public on all kinds of topics related to small business. Now, rightly so, Agora is adding Internet marketing to its offerings.

Attending Agora's new Internet seminar as an

observer reminded me of what a huge challenge it is to teach Internet marketing effectively, especially to beginners.

I think I've taken for granted what we've accomplished with The System over the years. After 12 years of teaching online marketing and working with and observing the progress of several thousand students, I've developed a feel for how to do it and things that are 'obvious' to me about the challenge involved are definitely not obvious to people just getting started in the teaching arena.

You rarely do...

One of the biggest mistakes in teaching any subject is to expose beginning students to challenging, advanced material before they're comfortable with the basics and can place the new knowledge in a context.

One invited guest speaker did this and you could see the energy and enthusiasm drain out of the room. I could practically 'hear' people in the audience saying to themselves "This Internet marketing thing isn't for me. I'm in way over my head." A real shame, because for people who understand direct marketing, the Internet should be as easy as falling off a log.

To help the students regain the sense of hopefulness they brought to the seminar, I told them the story of Sam Walton, the founder of Wal-Mart. As you may know, the Walton family is – by far – the richest family in the world. As a group, they actually make Bill Gates look poor and it would be hard to imagine a more sophisticated business operation than Wal-Mart's.

Sam Walton's original business dream was to own a <u>single</u> variety store. He and his wife found a location and poured their heart and soul into making it a success – and it was. Unfortunately, he didn't understand the terms of the lease he signed. It allowed his landlord to boot him out at any time, which his landlord promptly did, after he made it successful, so that he could start his own variety store at the same location with his son in charge.

Obviously, the Walton family recovered from this mishap… Now theoretically, Sam Walton could have prevented this early business catastrophe by getting it right the first time. But here's the reality: No one gets everything right the first time and no amount of preliminary study is going to make you into a Sam Walton - because even Sam Walton wasn't Sam Walton when he got started.

And here are the important words: <u>He got started</u>. He started with a small project that he could understand and even though he got it wrong the first time, things worked out fine because he was <u>in motion</u>.

OK, I Admit It, I'm Obsessed… More about Internet Video

I call it "The Archive." What it is really is a semi-organized walk-in closet packed floor to ceiling with the remnants of all kinds of Internet stuff I've been involved with over the years.

One of my prized possessions in the Archive is my complete collection of issues of "The Internet Gazette" – all four of them.

"The Internet Gazette" was an eight-page newspaper I published briefly in San Francisco in late 1994 and early 1995. It was a real newspaper by the way, not a Kinko's job. Each edition had 25,000 copies. I know. I personally loaded the truck myself when each new issue came out. (Those were the pre-spine injury days.)

Anyway, I was looking at the Gazette the other day and what do you think I put on the cover of the premier issue published in October of 1994?

Two articles: One about the threat of downloadable music to the music industry entitled "The Music Industry is Dead. Long Live Music."

The other? You guessed it: Video on the Internet.

"Are you crazy Ken?"

I remember the incredulity of multimedia whiz Hank Duderstadt who I commissioned to write the article. "You want me to write about THAT? Why? No one can do it."

My answer: "But someday people will be able to and when they can it will be the most powerful thing on the Internet. Let's be ready."

Among other things, Hank's article contained bits of practical advice like this: "Playing back a four mega-byte video clip can take almost half an hour with a typi-cal 14.4 bps modem."

And this: "There are few tasks to rival the frustra-tion of trying to get a decent-looking video to playback on a computer screen."

So you see, video on the Internet has been an obsession of mine for quite a while.

Now's the time

For reasons too complex to go into here, I believe Internet video is on the verge of the mother of all breakouts.

When it reaches critical mass, it's going to have a profound effect on the way the Internet is used to sell. We've already seen the Internet go from 'black and white' text, to text with color illustrations, to text with sound. This next wave could be the most laden with opportunity.

If want to watch this wave closely as it forms and follow developments in Internet video, go to my blog on the subject http://www.SystemVideoBlog.com

Note: This article was originally published in the fall of 2005.

Round Pegs in Square Holes

This summer I took a skills and aptitude test and got some very eye opening results.

Apparently, out of the thousands of people who've taken this test over the last twenty plus years, I'm one of only six who's ever scored so high on the unconventional thinker scale.

Needless to say, I never studied to be an unconventional thinker. In fact, just to show you how blind we can be to our own aptitudes, I never considered myself unconventional in my thinking at all.

But it sure explains a lot, doesn't it? For example, it explains why I'm often the first person to do something in the Internet marketing world. It also explains why I often don't do the smart thing, which is to take an already existing idea and work it over and squeeze every last nickel out of it. I'm more interested in the next thing that no one sees.

So far, being unconventional has made for a very interesting life. But it has had its frustrations.

I often see changes and new directions in Internet marketing with complete clarity months - and even years - before anyone else which means I'm often hanging out alone (perceptually speaking) and misunderstood.

For example, I was one of the first people to realize the Web had any commercial potential at all. I was one of the first people to realize the Internet was primarily a direct marketing medium. I was one of the first to see the testing and research potential in pay-per-click advertising. Not only did people not see these potentials at the time, I was often argued with and sometimes ridiculed for putting these ideas forward.

That's why the System and the System Club has been such a blessing to me. I've had receptive people to share my "crazy" ideas with. One of the benefits of being a System Club member is Club members get access to insights and resources that are not only ahead of the curve, they're not on anyone else's radar screen yet.

Being successful is not about aping someone else's success path

When I counsel people about their businesses, I always tell them there are a million ways to make money; so in reality, making money is not the issue. The real issue is making money in a way that fits with who you are, what you're good at, what you enjoy doing, what you do easily that no one else can do.

I also counsel people who are overextended with the following phrase which I coined before the US sent troops to the Middle East: "You can't invade Afghanistan with a pick up truck." In other words, your resources need to match your aspirations.

Having great aspirations is fine, but if you have them you need to develop a correspondingly grand set of resources through education, networking, out sourcing, etc. Or you may decide to scale back on your idea so that it fits the level of resources and infrastructure you're comfortable with building and managing.

Either way is fine. But whatever you do, follow the old Frank Sinatra song and do it your way. There's no need to contort yourself to enjoy success.

Direct
Marketing

Direct Mail Is Cool - Part One

I used to make ALL my money from direct mail and other forms of offline advertising.

I had to. There was no other way of reaching customers in the pre-Internet days.

And as much as I love the Internet, I have to say that...

Mail is cool

Mail has many incredible features:

1. It's **tangible**
2. It's **targetable**
3. It lets you **tell** your whole story

Are you worried about your customers receiving important communications from you? Good! You should be. E-mail is still the marketing wonder of the age, but in the era of overload and spam filters, the reality is your customers will miss messages from you. And even when your message is delivered perfectly, it may end up in the "I'll read it later file" i.e. in the virtual equivalent of the trash bin.

In contrast, mail gets attention. 98% of consumers bring their mail into their homes the same day it is delivered. 77% give it their immediate attention.

And instead of reading it at their computer, where distractions and potential interruptions are infinite, they read it in the comfort of their livings rooms (36%), kitchens (22%), studies (15%), bedrooms (8%) and dining rooms (8%.) They can do this because direct mail ads are <u>portable</u>. And - most important - the ad does not disappear when the computer is switched off. Direct mail is **tangible**.

The secret

If you segment your lists - physical or electronic - you get to take advantage of the most powerful force in advertising: **targeting**.

In a following chapter, I talk about the 40-40-20 rule which is the foundation of direct marketing success. It states that the ad itself only counts for about 20% of a campaigns success. Far more important is the message-to-market match, sending the right message to the right person. It counts for 80% of a campaign's success.

People who claim their letters 'sell' are only telling 20% of the story. Smart marketers pay a huge amount of attention to the other 80% and direct mail lets you play that advantage like a violin.

Finally, mail lets you **tell** your whole story. Postage and printing are not insignificant expenses, but as the direct mail old timers who instructed me liked to say: "Ink is cheap." Which means you can pack a lot of sales arguments into a 42 cent letter.

Also, today, with CDs and DVDs becoming practically dirt cheap to produce, you can not only take your message to the living room, you can also embed it in your customers DVD or CD player. Short of a live, personal visit, it doesn't get much better than that.

Direct Mail Is Cool - Part Two

Direct mail can mean anything from a dentist sending a 'courtesy reminder' postcard to an elaborate multi-hundred dollar package sent to a CEO.

Here's my advice if you're just starting out in direct mail: keep it simple and grab the low hanging fruit.

Low hanging fruit #1 - Package inserts

How would you like to mail for free with a virtual 100% guarantee that your prospect will read your ad?

There is a way and they're called package inserts.

There are two kinds of inserts: one you buy in order to get placement in another company's package and one you get for free by inserting them in your <u>own</u> packages. Which one do you think is the low hanging fruit?

If you ever order anything from a serious, high volume mailer (or someone with high volume experience), you will not only always find an ad inside the package, you'll very often find an ad for something <u>exponentially</u> more expensive than what you originally bought.

Why? Are these mailers crazy?

No. They know that that first purchase is a golden time. The prospect was excited enough to respond to your offer. They are anxiously awaiting their product. When it arrives, it's a bit like Christmas. You'll rarely find a better selling climate (assuming you deliver fast and the product is a "Wow!")

I have seen some companies successfully up sell from $49 to $5,000 just from a package insert. Now, granted, you don't get a lot of conversions, but a conversion rate of just <u>half of one percent</u> means an instant 50% boost to sales. Total marketing cost? Inserting a few extra pages in a box you're already paying to ship anyway.

This bit of advice may have just paid for the next ten years of System Seminars for you.

Low hanging fruit #2 –
Solo mailings to big buyers

Using the mail to prospect (i.e. turn cold prospects into leads or customers) is a tough game and I recommend you hold off on that for a while.

In contrast, mailing offers to existing customers is like shooting fish in a barrel. No, you probably won't get the same off-the-wall financial returns you get from e-mailing your customers, but you will sell more product, book more profits, and create a tighter bond with your customers.

If you're involved in a big promotion, at a minimum send a postcard to your best customers to reinforce your sales message. It's fast and cheap and there are services (including one offered by the US Post Office) that make it almost as easy as sending out e-mail.

Post cards are good, but full blown direct mail packages are better. More on that next…

Direct Mail Is Cool - Part Three

This is the last in a three part series on direct mail.

Part One was about the power of direct mail and why you should consider it. Part Two was about two simple, practically risk-free ways to use the mail to make money. Part Three is about how to create a winning direct mail package.

Ink is cheap

The most important principle to remember when it comes to creating direct mail packages is that "ink is cheap. "

What do I mean by that?

Postage is expensive. Paper is expensive. You can do a lot of common sense things to keep these costs down, the most important being to keep your list clean and updated so you're not mailing to bad addresses.

But once you've committed to a mailing, PACK the envelope. Get your full 42 cents worth of postage and makes sure every single piece of paper you put in the letter works hard for you.

You might notice that there isn't a lot of 'arty' white space in direct mail ads. The reason is simple. Every square inch of paper costs money to print and mail, but ink is cheap. For all practical purposes, it costs nothing to add more words.

Along the same lines, if you weigh your package before you mail it - and you should! - and there is room for more stuff, put it in. If there is room for an extra sheet of paper, use it. If there's room, for just a third of a piece of paper (known as a 'buck slip'), use it.

The package

Here are the basic elements that belong in every direct mail package: 1) a sales letter and 2) a stand-alone order form.

The order form first - literally.

In the old days, some direct mail people used to write the order form first. It's that important because it's the last thing your reader sees as he or she is about to make the purchase. Put your order form on a full sized piece of paper. Print only on one side of the paper. Recap the entire letter - key sales points, guarantees, description of bonuses - on the order form.

The sales letter. Again use regular 8 1/2 x 11 paper. White paper is fine. Your letter should look and read like a letter with one important exception: It must have a headline. Forget using a letterhead. It's generally a waste of precious selling space unless you're part of a famous organization like Harvard University.

Sounds simple? It is. There are, of course, fine points you can learn from books and studying great mailers like Rodale and Bottom Line, but this single page - short as it is - covered all the essentials.

Ed Mayer. Do you recognize the name?

My guess is 999 out of 1,000 Internet marketers don't.

Ed was famous for three things: 1) being a wickedly good direct marketer, 2) promoting quality direct marketing education tirelessly (he founded the first formal direct marketing program in the world at NYU) and 3) railing against the phonies and frauds who dragged the industry's reputation down.

Ed was, above all, a genius at formulating marketing principles and making them crystal clear. One of the biggest contributions he ever made to direct marketing was his 40-40-20 Rule.

The most important rule in direct marketing

The most dramatic and visible part of a direct marketing campaign, whether on the Internet or offline, is the ad copy.

Now, ad copy is extremely important. There's no doubt about that. All other things being equal, the prize goes to the person who writes the best ad.

But the reality is 'all other things' are rarely equal.

Let's take a look at a very simple example that will make this clear.

Two copywriters...one writes a so-so ad. The other writes a brilliant ad.

Two lists...one is made up of proven, hyper-responsive buyers who've been 'primed' to respond favorably to the offer. The other is an undifferentiated list of opt-ins.

Who's going to win?

The reality is that the so-so letter to the hyper-responsive list is going to wipe the floor with the brilliant letter sent to the so-so list.

Mayer broke it down this way: 40% of your success comes from having the right audience for your message, 40% comes from having the right offer for the audience, and 20% of your success comes from 'the creative'.
Richard Sears, the Great Grandfather of Direct Marketing, put it this way (and I'm paraphrasing):

"I can write the ad on a paper bag in crayon, but if it's the right offer for the right person at the right time, it will sell."

So what's the message here? That ad copy doesn't matter? No, not at all.

But a sales letter or web site - no matter how brilliantly conceived - can't overcome the wrong offer to the wrong list. As the late great Dick Benson used to say: "No one spends enough time on their lists and offers."

The All Important Follow-Up

"Be sure that your follow-up system is bringing you the maximum results...Maybe you can make changes in your letters - possibly you could add a letter or two making different propositions, etc. - that would make your follow-up letters more effective...

Your follow-up letters should not merely serve as reminders. Each letter should talk about your proposition from a different standpoint or emphasize some feature or features not so strongly emphasized in the other letters."

Great advice, isn't it?

It comes from a book called 'How to Make More Money' written by Louis Guenther.

Now here's the amazing part... Guenther first published this advice in 1907!

Who was this guy?

I asked System grad Phil Alexander - who is considered one of the world's leading authorities on the history of direct response - if he'd ever seen this book and he said it was new to him. From a cursory search on the Internet today, it appears to be a very, very rare book indeed.

I did some research and discovered that Guenther is best known for founding a publication called 'Financial World' which operated from 1902 to 1998. Among other things, he pioneered the practice of publishing stock ratings. The two guys who founded Forbes and Barron's respectively learned the financial reporting business from him as employees.

But in 1907, he focused his considerable business savvy with laser beam-like intensity on the then-developing world of 'selling by mail.'

It's astonishing how much of what appears in this 1907 book is 100% applicable today.

For example, his recommendations on how to write ad copy are among the best I've ever seen. Plus his advice on product selection, including a very detailed category-by-category analysis of what products and services have the potential to sell well via mail order, has uncanny relevance to Internet marketing.

The lessons

Two big lessons here...

First, the guys who created the mail order industry were a pretty savvy bunch and virtually all of what they learned is directly applicable to selling online, so if you're looking for inspiration or the proverbial 'kick in the pants,' salvation may be no further away that your local library or used book store.

Second, Guenther built a HUGE publishing company that thrived for nearly 100 years - and he was a nut for 'following up.' Are you following up with your prospects and customers? Can you do better? I bet you can and it's a good place to focus your energy. Here's some advice from Ken McCarthy: "If you want to make more money, follow up more."

The Care and Maintenance of Your Most Important Asset

At the end of every week, I take the latest version of my customer list to the bank and put it in my safety deposit box. There's an obvious practical reason for this - and a psychological one too.

The practical reason is that accidents can happen - power surges, hard drive crashes, burglaries, fires, freak storms - all things that can result in the loss of your data. The <u>psychological</u> reason for this weekly ritual is that it's a constant and vivid reminder to me that my customer list <u>is</u> my business.

Lists are living things

There's another important reason for my <u>weekly</u> deposit. It's a constant reminder to me that lists require <u>ongoing</u> care and attention. Every Friday, on the way to the bank, I ask myself "What have I done to enrich my list members this week?"

Why this unusual question? Because if I'm enriching my list members on a regular, ongoing basis, they will read what I have to say and be far more likely to act on offers I put in front of them.

This may seem like blazingly obvious common sense - and it is - but it's a surprisingly uncommon approach.

Value, value, and more value

There are two things that are true when it comes to lists: 1) You always want to be adding new names to them and 2) You always want to be bringing new value to the relationship. These two activities <u>combined</u> are what makes lists valuable and why they deserve the protection of a banker's vault.

Getting more names is pretty obvious, but making your names more valuable may not be.

Here's the secret:

If you think of the people on your list as <u>people</u> and not as an undifferentiated mass that you can hurl any-old-junk at, you will <u>naturally</u> do the right thing with your lists. For example:

You'll constantly be on the look out for useful and interesting information to send them on a regular basis...

When you evaluate potential offers, your first and last consideration will be the quality and value of the product or service you're recommending...

In short, you'll put the interest of your list members above your own short-term interests.

Doing these things <u>automatically</u> leads to higher response rates and increases the lifetime value of your customers. It's <u>real</u> wealth building, not 'hit and run' marketing.

What happens when a list is well cared for...

A month ago, I came across a truly first rate search engine marketing course produced by two guys who truly walk their talk. I sent out several mailings letting the people on my lists know about it.

The publisher contacted me a few weeks later and told me, in excited tones, that the conversion rate of the people I sent to their site was <u>exponentially</u> <u>higher</u> than all the other Internet marketing experts they had ever dealt with - "in a class by itself" as he put it.

And as it turned out, I not only had a better conversion rate, but I also made more - in absolute terms - than all their other JV partners.

In summary, to re-purpose a phrase from John F. Kennedy, if you really want to maximize the long-term value of your business "Ask not what your list can do for you, but what you can do for your list." With the vision and good sense to think and act this way, you'll be building yourself a solid, lucrative business that will last and produce wealth for a long time to come.

List Rot - Causes and Cures...

How many times have you heard someone brag about the size of their list?

I've dealt with many multi-hundred thousand name list owners over the last ten years and I can tell you I've been frequently <u>under</u>-whelmed by their responsiveness.

What's the problem?

Actually, it's <u>many</u> problems.

Because e-mail is a fantastically inexpensive and forgiving medium, a lot of Internet marketers - including many acclaimed 'superstars' - have failed to learn some of the most basic lessons of list management.

'List management.' It sounds boring and dry, doesn't it?

Well, consider this: If your list is the lifeblood of your business, doesn't it make sense that list management should be something more that loading all your e-mail addresses into a file and pressing send every now and then?

Fact of life: Lists rot. People move, they change addresses, your domain gets added to their spam filter, and worst of all - they lose interest.

They lose interest because you've ignored them for too long, or you've sent too much of the 'same old, same old.' Lists are pretty forgiving, but those are two failings that are hard to recover from.

Solutions

#1 - **Be aware**. Simply reminding yourself - every day - that an untended list will rot is an important step towards preventing and treating the problem. (Yes, list rot <u>is</u> a preventable disease.)

#2 - **Mail**. Never let a month go by without mailing something of value to your list. (In the print world, quarterly newsletters are hard to make work. For some reason, human beings need a monthly exposure - at a minimum - to stay connected.)

#3 - **Mail more often**. Few Internet marketers fail on the side of mailing too often. Yes, there are some folks who seem to be members of the 'get rich quick' offer-of-the-day club, but, in fact, they are few and far between. I am on two lists that send me stuff <u>every</u> single day - sometimes more that once a day - and more often then not I read every single issue. In fact, their e-mail is a highlight of my day.

#4 - **Mail value - <u>always</u>**. You don't have to mail every day, but you do have to make sure that everything you mail is <u>packed</u> with value. Ask yourself: "Is this good enough to merit my reader interrupting his day." It better be, because if it's not, it may be the last thing of yours he ever reads. (It pays to be a little paranoid.)

#5 - **Use change-ups**. Don't mail the same old thing every time. Surprise your readers from time to time. The ideal state of mind you want to induce in your readers is that when your e-mail arrives they ask themselves: "I wonder what he's up to now?"

The New Publishing Paradigm

(This is the second time I've used the word 'paradigm' in two weeks, but hey, 'if the shoe fits...')

Publishing has gone through a radical revolution in the past twenty years.

Not long ago, 'publishing' meant going on bended knee to a New York publishing house and begging them to put your book in print.

In the 1980s, desktop publishing liberated self-publishers from the need for expensive typesetters, and self-publishing - always a quiet, steady rumble, in the background - turned into a roaring movement.

Just a decade later, the Internet came along dissolved another obstacle to self-publishing - distribution - and hundreds of millions of web pages, and countless eBooks, were born.

Now what?

In a word: Glut. You see it on the Internet. You see it in any one of the thousands of super-sized book stores that has cropped up in the last decade. You even see it on newsstands. System Club member and book publicity expert Kim Dushinski tells me that almost 200,000 new book titles come out each year.

For the person who has a point of view he or she wants to share with the world, it has never been more important to master the art of direct marketing.

Direct marketing, of which Internet marketing is a sub-category, can be simplified down into two activities: attracting customers and harvesting customer value.

That's it. There really is no more to it, but, of course, the devil is in the details.

In the old world of publishing, <u>all</u> the focus was on selling the book. After all, isn't that what the publishing business is all about? Being a published author, having a best seller, isn't that the pot at the end of the rainbow? With 200,000 new books coming out a year, the answer is a resounding "NO!"

Information services, lifelong customers, and true wealth

The world's smartest publishing companies - and there aren't that many of them - are starting to figure out that the book (or eBook) is only the beginning of the story, that the real prize is a relationship with the book buyer.

Relationship means repeat sales and repeat sales mean higher profits... <u>much</u> higher profits. What does it cost you to find and convert a new customer? Compare that with what it costs to sell to an existing customer. Now imagine a stream of future purchases from a single buyer. One happy customer can easily be worth five or ten new buyers in terms of bottom line profit.

Now imagine all the high end services that can be sold to book buyers - coaching, consulting, home study courses, workshops, memberships, certifications, equipment, travel packages etc. - I call these things 'information services.' Now a single customer can be worth 100 or even 1,000 book buyers.

The solution is in the problem

The 'problem' of 200,000 new books each year is not just a problem for publishers. It's a problem for info seekers as well. The reality of having an excessive number of choices is stressful and we live in a society of total choice overload: cell phone plans, cable TV packages, investment options. It seems like every time we enter into the simplest of transactions, we're faced with the need to have a PhD. in the subject before we can make a move.

And that's where you come in.

There is a great deal of money to be made in being the 'shining light', the beacon that info seekers can trust. The one who lets them shut out all the noise so they can make their decision with as little pain as possible and get on with their lives. Build your info business around being that person, and the money will flow.

I Learned It At the Movies...

Long ago, I was a partner in a start up film post-production company that was on the verge of going broke. Our company specialized in audio post-production: creating, acquiring and mixing the music, sound effects, and voice-overs to create the movie's sound tracks.

My partner was a technical genius, but he was a marketing moron. He spent all his time building an incredibly innovative digital audio editing system, but didn't do anything to market himself at all. Things were so bad that when I signed on, he was just a few weeks from closing the doors.

I didn't know a thing about movie making at the time, but I knew there was a market for what he offered and that we could reach it.

I wish I could say I was a marketing genius, but all I did was get a list of TV commercial producers and send them a postcard. It was enough to generate $17,000 in high margin business in less than 20 days and we were off the races. Within five years the company had an Academy Award winning film as a client and moved from a low rent, firetrap office into a Manhattan brownstone.

Ogilvy, Schwartz and Citizen Kane

One of the things I've noticed over the years is the impact the movie business has had on many of our greatest marketing minds.

For example: David Ogilvy's first job as a young man was working for the famous pollster George Gallup providing audience analysis services to Hollywood. It was while working for Gallup that he discovered that, on the average, movie goers need to hear a film mentioned seven times before they seriously considered seeing it.

Lesson: Expose your prospects to your offer more times and you'll make more money.

The great copywriter Eugene Schwartz used to advise his copywriting students to see every current movie with a box office of $100,000,000 or more. Why? For a movie to sell that many seats, it has to powerfully resonate with the public and generate strong word of mouth.

Lesson: Gene learned a lot from the formula the producers of the 'Lethal Weapon' series used: "Five minutes of dialog - a fist fight - five minutes of dialog - a car chase - five minutes of dialog - an explosion." In other words, punctuate your sales letters with fireworks on a regular basis. A great cure for what David Ogilvy called the worst sin in advertising... being dull.

William Randolph Hearst, the subject of Orson Welles' movie 'Citizen Kane,' was a massively successful print publisher and pioneering movie producer.

Though he was a highly unscrupulous man - he bragged about helping start the Spanish American War to improve the circulation of his newspapers - he was a phenomenal promoter.

One of Heart's biggest discoveries was "the cliff hanger," deliberately ending a movie at a point of high unresolved tension to lure movie goers back to the theater the following week.

Lesson: You make more money selling a series than from being a 'one-hit wonder.'

Movie promotion is a high stakes game. Take advantage of the blood, sweat and tears the industry pours into promoting its products, see a popular movie or two every now and then - and take notes.

Surveys – Misleading, Even Dangerous

"I don't have any focus groups on talent and programming. If I need five people in a mall to be paid $40 to tell me how to do my job, I shouldn't have my job." Roger Ailes, CEO of Fox News.

Like him or loathe him, no one can dispute that Roger Ailes has created a major hit – and, unlike his more timid competitors, he did it without surveys or focus groups.

Veteran Bob Bly, our System Club guest in August, wrote an article that was published in a recent issue of DM News with the provocative headline "Are Customer Surveys a Waste of Time?"

Bob's answer: Not a total waste of time, but highly overrated - and not without risk.

How to tank a business

Bob cites an article that appeared in the August issue of Business Week to back up his position.

Apparently, the Gap – one of the savviest clothing retailers in America – has lost its way. Sales are down 4% the last quarter alone and are projected to drop another 2% in the current quarter. For a company like the

Gap with it ferocious fixed overhead, this adds up to very serious numbers and alarming trend.

What went wrong?

In 2002, the company made a huge investment in focus groups, surveys, and other market research. Shouldn't that have resulted in <u>better</u> sales?

Not necessarily. Especially when marketers depend on survey responses to tell them what to do.

The consensus of eight Gap employees and two retail industry analysts: The Gap "has shifted too far toward research and away from the <u>instinct and emotion</u> favored by many successful clothing merchants." (Emphasis mine.)

Innovations don't come from survey results

Talking and listening to your customers always makes a lot of sense and to the extent that surveys help you do that, they're worthwhile, but to try to create a product or ad copy based on survey results is madness.

The motion picture industry is notorious for trying to survey their way to hit movies and they fail over and over again. Hit movies invariably come 'out of nowhere' and are produced by people with vision and passion.

As a marketer, you need to know your market, but you also need to <u>lead</u> you market. The fact of life is that your prospects don't sit around thinking in detailed ways about what would make a real difference in the marketplace. That's <u>your</u> job.

Survey children on what they'd like to eat for dinner and they'll tell you cotton candy and ice cream. Survey cavemen on what would improve their lives and they'd have told you 'bigger clubs.' Consumers didn't ask for the telephone, the automobile, the electric light bulb, or the Internet. These leaps came from people who cultivated vision.

Marketing 'gurus' in corporate America, in the direct marketing industry, and in the Internet world would like to have you believe that creating hit products can be reduced to buying their surveying services or software programs. Baloney.

I can't think of a single blockbuster hit in <u>any</u> market that was <u>ever</u> created with survey results as the raw material.

Copywriting

Writing Ad Copy - It's <u>Not</u> What You Think It Is

I've stayed out of the copywriting education business... until now.

But I'm getting into it for the same reason I got back in the Internet marketing education business in 2000. There's a TON of bad, misleading, and flat out stupid advice floating around out there about how to write ad copy and things seem to be getting worse, not better.

It's gotten so bad that lately some of the 'experts' have taken to offering seminars on copywriting that are designed not to deliver the goods, but to persuade you to pay them super-inflated fees for paint-by-numbers, assembly-line-style copy that they then farm out to copywriting 'newbies.'

It's time that <u>somebody</u> stepped up and took these bad practices on - and I guess that somebody is going to be me.

Here are the three big myths that dominate much of Internet copywriting 'education' today:

Myth # 1: Copywriting is about screaming in all caps, using multiple exclamation points, making wild promises (the more outlandish the better), and creating clever over-the-top phrases.

Myth #2: You don't have to create anything to be a copywriter. Just take someone else's work, re-write it a bit, slap your name on it and you're done. (Which is, in fact, how many of the Internet marketing 'gurus' produce their own copy.)

Myth #3: Copywriting is easy. Just send me $XXXX and I'll send you my secret formula.

Putting copywriting back on track

I'm going to neutralize these dangerous misconceptions with some <u>useful</u> reality...

Reality #1: There are no copywriting secrets

Yes, there are some instances where I would <u>gladly</u> spend several thousand dollars to hear the insights of a <u>true</u> top performer... and these folks are a lot rarer than you think... but, in fact, everything you need to know to write record-breaking sales pieces can be found in the classics, many of which are available for $20 or less.

Read them! Re-read them. And then re-read them again. Literally, soak your brain in them. And then write... every day. In truth, it <u>is</u> simple - but it's <u>not</u> easy. Copywriting requires 'elbow grease' and elbow grease is one thing you can't buy from the store or on the Internet. You've got to supply it yourself. There's no way around it.

Reality #2: 'Knock off' artists are losers not winners

Yes, you can save some time, and you might even make some money, ripping off the hard work of other people. There are even some Internet marketing 'gurus' - including one who is currently very popular - who will tell you that 'stealing' other people's ideas is <u>the</u> way to go.

But I've dealt with some of these people - behind the scenes - and I can tell you it's not a pretty sight.

The biggest challenge - and the biggest pay off - in marketing and advertising is to come up with a new way to present an 'old thing' - and that takes creative, fresh thinking.

(By the way, when I say an 'old thing,' I'm not talking about something inferior or 'worn out.'

People want to be richer, healthier, thinner, more attractive to the opposite sex, more impressive to their friends, more independent, have more time, do less work, feel better, have interesting experiences, raise successful kids etc. None of these things are new. These are the most ancient of drives. 'Old things.')

The <u>real</u> money in direct response advertising goes to the people who know how to breathe new life into these old themes. Knowing how to do this is a skill that you can learn and when you do, it will give you a <u>tremendous</u> amount of power because you'll become a <u>source</u> of new ideas and perspectives, not someone skulking around in the shadows looking for the next person to rip off.

Reality #3: In reality, great ad copy comes from passionate caring, not BS, hype, and con artistry.

No, I'm not trying to sell you a 'Hallmark-style feel-good' greeting card.

I'm talking about hard, cold business reality. The fact is, when it comes to selling, he who cares the most wins.

What do I mean by 'caring' in this context? I mean the following:

1. You <u>care</u> about the people who are prospects for your product or service.

2. You <u>care</u> that the product you're advertising does what it's supposed to do and is a good value.

3. You <u>care</u> that the existence of your product - your solution - makes it into the consciousness of as many of the people who need it as possible and you leave no stone unturned whether it's finding new media to reach the market or adding one more piece of persuasive information to your sales copy.

Model yourself after the pros, not the hacks

Great copywriting is not about being 'macho,' over-the-top, cynical, manipulative, or worldly-wise.

That's for hacks and 'knock off' artists.

These people like to think that they're 'outsmarting' their prospects. In reality, the only person they're outsmarting is themselves because in their mad rush to be 'clever' they are, more often then not, stepping over the real money - long term dollars - as they greedily run after today's pennies.

On a recent tele-seminar I did with Jay Abraham that focused on the work of one of the truly great ad writers, Eugene Schwartz, the question of the <u>funda-mental</u> <u>source</u> of great ad copy came up.

Jay recounted his legendary success with an anti-inflammatory product called 'Icy Hot.'

The moderator, copywriter Bob Bly, asked Jay what motivated him to take on the product in the first place and pour so much of his energy into it?

Jay said it was the big stack of unsolicited testimonial letters customers of the product had mailed the company over the years. In short, the product <u>really</u> worked and it relieved the intense suffering of people who were not able to find relief through any other means. Figuring out how to get this solution to the largest number of people became the focus of Jay's life at the time.

And that, in a nutshell, is how the real money is created in the marketplace...by caring.

<u>Real</u> Copywriting Wisdom

In this letter, I'd like to introduce one of the great past masters of advertising. For some reason, his work doesn't get much attention on the seminar circuit. In fact, I don't think I've ever heard his name mentioned even once in any of the marketing seminars I've attended over the last twenty-plus years.

Introducing William Bernbach...

When Americans were in love with huge cars with lots of chrome and space-age styling, William Bernbach persuaded them to take a serious look at a cramped, ugly looking car called 'The Beetle.' Thus was Volkswagen's market in the US born.

When Hertz dominated the rent-a-car market in the US and there was no way to equal their penetration, William Bernbach figured out how to make being #2 a virtue with "We Try Harder." And thus Avis grew overnight from an obscure, virtual non-entity into a powerhouse in the rent-a-car market.

The TRUTH about great ad copy

Sadly, these days a lot of people are peddling - and a lot of people are buying - the idea that copywriting is all about hyperbole, making wild promises, and bending - if not shredding - the truth.

The best and most successful ad writers take a totally different view.

Here's William Bernbach's formula for breakthrough advertising (edited a bit by me):

1. The most powerful element in advertising is the truth.

2. The truth isn't the truth until people believe you.

3. They can't believe you if they don't know what you're saying.

4. They can't know what you're saying if they don't listen to you.

5. They won't listen to you if you're not interesting.

6. You won't be interesting unless you say things imaginatively, originally, freshly.

7. Our job is to bring the dead facts to life.

To sum up William Bernach and every other truly effective copywriter I've ever met or studied, **successful advertising is nothing more - or less - than telling the truth about your product in a vivid, compelling, and inspiring way.**

Is this more work than the 'copy, paste, and smooth over' school of copywriting? You bet it is. But the extra effort more than pays off... Bernbach says it best: **"Practiced properly, creativity can make one ad do the work of ten."** Great copy is an amazing opportunity for leverage. It's worth the extra work.

In the two-day advanced copywriting training I gave in Miami in the winter of 2005, I had the opportunity to talk about some of the 'extra-copy' elements that go into creating great ad copy and building a successful info marketing businesses.

To make a very long story short, when you get to the very top of the copywriting tree, you find people who are what David Ogilvy used to call 'gentleman with brains.'

(He coined this phrase in the days before women took their place in the advertising world.)

Having had the opportunity to correspond with people like David Ogilvy and meet and talk at some length with people like Eugene Schwartz and Gary Bencinvenga, I can verify that the very best copywriters I've met all have a great deal of <u>real</u> empathy and respect for their prospects.

They are all also completely passionate and dedicated to their work.

If you've found work you feel passionate about, you know what a great gift it is. It's by no means a 'free ride,' but it is a qualitatively different experience than just business for the sake of business.

If you haven't quite found a focus for yourself yet, know that it is a very worthy quest and is one of the great challenges that face every human being.

I just came across a remarkable resource on this subject in the form of a book. It's called "What Should I Do with My Life?" and it's written by Po Bronson who spent years going down a countless number of blind alleys before he finally discovered his calling.

There are no answers in this book. No ten-step checklists either.

Instead it's an extremely intelligent, perceptive, and useful discussion of the nature of the challenge of finding your life's worth.

To write this book, Bronson analyzed his own life story and then talked with dozens of others about how they found - and it some cases had not yet found - a satisfying focus for their life's talents, interests and aspirations.

It's an absolutely brilliant piece of work and I strongly recommend it to everyone.

"What Should I Do with My Life?"

The answer to this question is, of course, entirely personal and it's nothing that can be learned from a book or a seminar, but Bronson's book offers a uniquely useful and valuable beacon.

My highest recommendation.

Note: The book has one minor flaw. A 'sharpie' named Deni Leonard conned Bronson into including in his book Leonard's mostly bogus account of his success as a businessman. It was one of those 'too good to be true' stories that turned out not to be. Such people unfortunately are not uncommon as Bronson found out the hard way. It happens.

Creative Energy, Sales and Business Building

For some strange reason 'creativity' has become a dirty word among many direct marketing and Internet marketing educators.

"Copy, borrow, steal, but NEVER create" seems to be the motto. One famous copywriting teacher advises students that the best way to write ad copy is to "copy, paste and smooth over." "Keep a big collection of other people's ads and when you need to write an ad for yourself, just change it a little to adapt it to your offer. "

Is this really good advice?

Yes and no

It's true that advertising novices, who don't have their eye firmly on the ball, often do get carried away with being creative, but no one reading this letter is likely to suffer from this problem.

It's also true that it is a tremendous help when you sit down to write an ad to have your unconscious mind packed with examples of winning ads.

But should you really throw creativity out the window and focus your energy on 'knocking off' other people's sales messages to build your business? I don't think so. In fact, I think it's really bad advice.

Am I saying that you can't make money with a "copy, paste and smooth over" strategy? No. Of course you can, but the biggest - and most stable - wins come to people who tell their <u>own</u> story, not a warmed over version of someone else's leftovers.

What works

When you look at the sales letters of the very top direct response copywriters of the last 30 years - people like Eugene Schwartz, Gary Bencivenga, and Gary Halbert - you won't smell even a whiff of the "copy-paste" formula at work.

You also won't see the kind of over-the-top, "this is the greatest ever!" kind of language that has become the norm for so many Internet-based copywriters.

What do these copywriters do instead?

They become <u>fascinated</u> by all of the details of the product they're selling. They become <u>enthusiastic</u> about all the good things it can do for the people who buy it. They become <u>determined</u> to demonstrate that it's an excellent value and something that the prospect can trust beyond all shadow of a doubt.

Selling - whether in person, in print, or via a computer screen - is the transference of information, enthusiasm and conviction from the mind of the salesperson to the mind of the buyer.

When the prospect first glances at your ad, he's like a dead battery. Only <u>one</u> thing is going to get him to 'turn over': the state of <u>your</u> battery.

To 'jump start' your prospect's enthusiasm, you've got to create it in yourself <u>first</u> and the best way to create it is by caring - really caring - about your prospect and being absolutely convinced that the product you're offering is the right thing for him. That's hard to do with a "copy, paste, and smooth over" approach to business.

Correct Form vs. 'Fire'

I've been writing ad copy in one form or another for thirty years. I started when I was 15 long before I ever heard the term 'ad copy' or thought of myself as a copywriter.

Over the last fifteen years I've given a lot of thought to how to help people write their own winning ads.

I used to think that if folks learned the classic principles and formulas and applied themselves to their work that ultimately they'd be able to achieve the same results that I and other top copywriters do.

Now I'm not so sure. There's something beyond 'formal correctness' that makes successful ads work.

This past year, I made an intense study of the inner core of copywriting to answer this question:

Why does some copy 'crash and burn' while other copy goes to the moon?

In my search, I re-read the classics; I reviewed my own very successful sales letters and those of other people; I had the rare opportunity to speak at length with Gary Bencivenga, one of the copywriting world's true greats...all these things helped, but none of them gave me the answer I was looking for.

Ironically, it was <u>bad</u> ads and bad sales letters that provided me with what I was seeking.

There are two kinds of bad ads. The first kind is <u>obviously</u> bad: no headline, confusing copy, no call to action. Beginner's mistakes.

The other kind of 'bad ad' is a little harder to pin down. Everything that's supposed to be there <u>is</u> there. Big headline. Lots of bullet points. Testimonials. Clear call to action. Correct in every sense of the word, but the overall effect is as appealing as a dead fish that's been left in the sun too long.

The noteworthy thing is that while some of these 'bad' letters come from students who are learning copywriting, many of them come from professionals including some 'name' copywriters I've hired to help me with my workload. In every case, I've had to reject their work and do it myself which makes me wonder...

Am I being too hard on these guys?

I don't think so. There's a phrase in the entertainment industry that describes a performance that's technically correct, but lacking in fire: "He phoned it in."

That's how a lot of the copy I'm seeing these days reads. Phoned in. Technically correct, but lackluster.

<u>Fire</u> is not something achieved with screaming headlines, exclamation points, or lifetime guarantees. Those things are, at best, props. Fire comes from being so excited about what your product does for people that you're afraid you'll burst if you don't tell them about it. Not <u>saying</u> you feel this way. <u>Really</u> feeling this way.

Guess who the most likely person on earth is to write copy about your product that has real fire in it?

<u>YOU</u>...and it's a lot easier for you to learn how to organize your customer and product knowledge into a compelling sales letter than it is to find, educate and motivate an outside writer to do it for you.

It took me a lot of time, money and effort to figure this out. Here's hoping you learn from my experience.

Home at Last

I've been on the road continuously since May 3. It's good to be home. In some ways, this whole year has been like a homecoming to me.

As anyone who has been my student for a while knows, I've spent the last 15 years (and yes there are Club members who were clients long <u>before</u> the Internet) singing the praises of people like Gene Schwartz, Dick Benson, Gary Bencinvenga and the brilliants folks at Rodale, Boardroom and Agora.

Until this year, it was a pretty lonely stand - especially in the Internet world.

I'd talk about the incredible accomplishments of these folks and how much there was to learn from them and I'd watch people's eyes glaze over. The 'gurus' were especially disinterested. I guess their reasoning was since there was no way to make a buck off these greats, why tell people about them?

12 months that shook the world

Well, that's all changing. The 'sleeping giants' are awakening.

A year ago, Boardroom brought Gene Schwartz's masterpiece "Breakthrough Advertising" back into print.

Agora shined a bright light on it with a home study course and they were kind enough to invite me to co-teach the first lesson with Jay Abraham.

Gary Bencivenga granted his first - and still his only - interview ever - for System Club members only.

Boardroom just re-released Dick Benson's essential classic "Secrets of Successful of Direct Mail" which has been on my Top Five Must-Read Book List since the day it was published.

And the cherry on top of the sundae was this past weekend in New York City: The long awaited (20 years for me) Gary Bencivenga seminar.

Gary, for those of you who may not know, has been the world's most highly regarded direct mail copywriter for many years. Until last summer, he'd never shared the details of his copywriting methods with anyone - and last weekend in New York City he opened the floodgates.

Good company

I was delighted to see so many System Club members at this seminar. We made up over 10% of the room.

Interestingly, there were no Internet 'gurus' in the audience. But Gary Halbert and John Carlton were there - as fully paid attendees - taking notes as fast as they could write. And Boardroom, Agora, Phillps, KCI and

Rodale - which together produce over half a BILLION dollars in sales per year - were well represented as was the elite corps of the world's top freelance copywriters who keep their promotional engines running.

If you missed it, don't despair. As a System Club member you're one of a select handful of people who receive the CDs of the extended interview I did with Gary last summer. It's solid gold. <u>And only System Club members have it</u>.

Finding the Right Tone

If you've been studying the Gary Bencivenga CDs and/or attended Gary's seminar in New York two weekends ago, you might have been surprised to notice that the world's most highly regarded direct response copywriter does <u>not</u> pour on the hype when he sets out to sell something.

Clearly, the core of powerful advertising is making a dramatic promise, but that does <u>not</u> automatically translate into making wild, 'frothing-at-the-mouth' claims.

Now, if your audience is made up of people who have the mentality of professional wrestling fans and you've trained them to expect over-the-top hyperbole from you, then have at it. But most marketplaces are made up of <u>normal</u> people who are naturally skeptical and who run at the first sign of hype and BS.

The Middle Way approach

System Club member, Robert Middleton has built a successful business teaching professionals how to profitably market their professional services. Over the years, he's observed three basic approaches people take to marketing themselves.

It's very common for business people to grossly <u>undersell</u> themselves. Some 'gurus' recommend that they fix this error by aggressively <u>overselling</u> themselves. Neither approach is terribly effective for building a solid business.

Instead of hiding one's light under a bushel or blowing one's own horn to a preposterous degree, Robert recommends seeking The Middle Way in contrast with what he calls 'Hiding' and 'Sleazoid' marketing. Here are some examples he offers of how these three different types approach common marketing challenges:

Hiding: I'm just grateful my clients use my services at all.

Sleazoid: My clients are suckers waiting to be fleeced.

Middle Way: The relationship with my clients is one of mutual respect.

Hiding: I don't want to be pushy about what I recommend.

Sleazoid: All my clients buy my biggest package whether they need it or not.

Middle Way: I will make recommendations that are based on what I can really deliver.

Hiding: I'm not really sure what my clients want or need.

Sleazoid: I know what my clients need better than they do.

Middle Way: I work to understand the needs and concerns of my clients.

Hiding: People really don't want to know about my services.

Sleazoid: If you can't dazzle them with brilliance, baffle them with bull---t.

Middle Way: I need to educate my prospective clients about what I do.

Robert's modest, even-tempered Middle Way approach may strike folks who've been indoctrinated in the 'scream-as-loud-as-you-can' school of marketing as weak. It's anything but.

As Gary pointed out so eloquently at his seminar and as his career testifies to, prospects and customers have well developed BS detectors, are quick to 'turn the channel' at the first sign of empty boasting, and are responsive - <u>very responsive</u> - to being talked to like intelligent, perceptive people.

Endless Improvement

System Club member John Rinaldi sent me an e-mail last week about a program he overheard on TV. Producer Cameron McIntosh and composer Andrew Lloyd Weber were talking about the secret behind the success of their phenomenon "Phantom of the Opera". Here's what he heard (paraphrased):

"...Musicals like this are not written as much as they are rewritten. The process is one of successive enhancement, continuously discarding, modifying and replacing pieces until it works right..."

John offered this commentary:

"I jumped up when I heard that. Doesn't that sound exactly like the process that you describe for copywriting? It probably applies to life in general. To get good at anything we do a process of successive refinement until we are satisfied with the outcome."

'Instant' sells - but reality is different

Few people like to hear the word 'work' so when it's time to sell something, it pays to put emphasis on the 'fast, easy and quick' aspects of your offer.

As copywriting ace Gene Schwartz once pointed out, every good product <u>does</u> offer some instant improvement even if all of the improvements it offers are not instant. (He very sagely called his publishing company **Instant Improvement.)**

But, reality - as I'm sure you've noticed - doesn't always permit improvements to be instant.

For example, ten years ago last month, I was in an accident that left me physically disabled for several years. Everything was painful. Walking was difficult, sleep was fitful at best, and I was only able to carry a small fraction of my previous workload. Ten years later, there are still a lot of things I can't do like run (something I used to love to do) or lift anything over 25 pounds, but every year things get a little better and I'm optimistic that someday I'll be able to run again.

Part of my improvement process involves two one-and-a-half hour sessions every week with a gifted exercise physiologist. She knows exactly how the muscles of the body weave and work together and exactly what to do to bring them back into strength and balance. In my case, it's been a long process, but the work is definitely paying off, slow as it is.

"It's beautiful"

Two weeks ago, we lost one of the great innovators in the world of street-smart, bootstrap Internet marketing, Corey Rudl. Looking through my archives, I found a tape of an interview that I'd done with him in 2001 at a conference in Colorado where we met for the first time. You can listen to it by going to this page: http://www.thesystemseminar.com/corey

One of the things that jumped out at me while listening to this interview was how often Corey used the word 'beautiful.' Pretty unusual after all when what he was talking about was WORK.

Listening to this interview, you can't fail to be impressed by the sheer amount of time, effort and energy Corey poured into his various enterprises over the years - the ones that didn't work as well as the ones that did.

Here was a person who was clearly in love with the process of making things better. In his case that meant selling more auto parts (his first business), then selling more books about cars online (his second business), then finally, what became his life's work, teaching what he'd learned to small business people so they could profit from the Internet too.

It is beautiful to work at something with all your heart. It's also happens to be the only way I know to 'motivate' yourself to do all the things that are required to succeed. Endless improvement. That's what it's all about.

The Invisible Foundation of 'Killer' Ad Copy

One of the surprise bonuses I offered attendees at last winter's Advanced Copy and Info Marketing seminar was a half hour consultation with me on their ad copy.

This has been tremendously educational for <u>me</u>.

You see, I already know how to write ad copy. In fact, I've even received fan mail from people like Gary Bencivenga and Boardroom's Marty Edelston. What I don't know completely yet is how to help other people become 'killer' copywriters too. It's a learning process and I work as hard at it as anybody.

Opening the door to serious students who've been through my hard core training has given me a priceless opportunity to see the things about writing ad copy that I take for granted.

Most promotions for ad copy training focus on the glamorous stuff, the fireworks and that's great, but I've discovered that a lot of folks are so new to copywriting that they're missing what I call the 'invisible foundation.'

Ads don't live in a vacuum

Brilliant words are not what win the day.

Clarity and relevance backed by emotion - <u>after</u> credibility is established - is what makes the cash register ring.

I see a lot of folks trying to be clever and crafty with their ads. Big mistake. Huge mistake. <u>Fatal</u> mistake.

Instead start - and finish - by asking yourself these three questions:

1. <u>Who</u> is going to be reading this ad?

2. <u>What</u> do I want the reader to DO as the result of reading this letter?

3. <u>What</u> does this person already know - about me? about my product? about the problem this product solves?

Blazingly obvious?

Maybe these three questions appear to be too simple to consider, but again and again I review letters where the writer has not fully thought these questions out.

These are THE questions. In fact, if you strip down Eugene Schwartz's highly complex and sophisticated classic "Breakthrough Advertising" it all boils down to systematically analyzing these three questions.

Copywriting pyrotechnics are cool and tricks of the trade are fun and well worth studying, but when you read the letters that have kicked proverbial 'butt' in the marketplace, invariably you'll find logic, clarity, thoroughness, and a kind of 'plain speaking' that's somehow manages to be both confidence inspiring and fascinating at the same time.

It pays to be simple.

In Memory of Ed McLean
(1927 – 2005)

He was a crackerjack copywriter, one of the best that ever was - and certainly one of the most prolific with over 9,000 mailings, print ads, radio spots, and publication inserts under his belt.

He was an inspired educator too. In 1967, he was the first person to design a college level course for direct response copywriting and was one of the founders of the Direct Marketing Writers Guild, a group that helped countless fledgling copywriters get a toehold in the industry.

And he was a great guy: generous, encouraging, intelligent and independent... Ed McLean.

Selling the unsellable

If you're steeped in direct marketing lore, you've probably heard the story about the Mercedes diesel.

Mercedes Benz made a serious miscalculation about the number of 1967- era Americans who'd be interested in their diesel sedan. Big sellers in Europe, they were virtually unknown to American consumers and the company was lucky to sell a few thousand a year.

One year, someone sent way too many to the states and Mercedes called David Ogilvy to help bail them out.

Who did Ogilvy call on to fix the point on the spear (write the sales letter?) Ed McLean.

The result? $3,500,000.00 worth of these strange, noisy, foreign cars were sold with a six-page sales letter. Total sales cost: less than $100,000. (Postage was just eight cents then.)

The trick was giving buyers a creative rebate. In this case, a year's worth of diesel fuel. In those days that amounted to $120 for 12,000 miles traveled. Small change for a car that sold for $4,068.00 (Yes, there's been some inflation since 1967.)

Helping the next generation

Ed had the perfect background for writing direct response ad copy: He was in love with writing and was an aspiring novelist (like Eugene Schwartz, Dan Kennedy, and Mark Ford, just to name a few.)

And he served time as a door-to-door salesman, first selling pots and pans in New Orleans and then baby photos in Brooklyn. After being bit twice on the same ankle by two different dogs in a two-week stretch, he decided to get off the street and get a real job.

Hired by Newsweek at the age of 32, he hit the ball out of the park with the very first direct mail letter he ever wrote. It became Newsweek's control, ran for an incredible 17 years and was reportedly received by more than 150 million people.

I remember Ed for his keen mind and generosity. He used to write a regular column for the DM News and in exchange received a small ad that included his mailing address in Ghent, NY (coincidentally not far from where I live now.) One day, when the idea of me ever succeeding in direct marketing seemed as remote as me flying to the moon, I took a chance and wrote him a letter.

He wrote back! And thus began a regular correspondence in the pre-email days. I can't tell you how much that meant to me at the time. David Ogilvy had a name for people like Ed McLean: "gentlemen with brains." A great ad writer and a great guy. He'll be missed by many.

Business and Marketing Advice

How to Enroll In the World's Greatest Marketing University

One of the major downsides of formal education is that it trains a lot of people to think that 'real' learning only takes place in school and that all worthwhile information comes from 'authorities.'

Nothing could be further from the truth.

In fact, I'd venture to say that 99%+ of all the useful things we learn we learn when we're not in a classroom and there are no teachers around. This is especially true in marketing and business.

Everyday life is, quite literally, the greatest marketing university you could ever possibly attend. The lessons just keep coming non-stop, around the clock, day in and day out... if you're awake to them.

For example, one day, many years ago, a fast food executive drove up to the drive-in teller of his bank and asked: "This works so well for banking. I wonder if it would work for our restaurants?"

The answer is it works great. Today, approximately one third of all fast food transactions take place at drive-in windows. That adds up to an enormous amount of money, certainly billions of dollars per year. And all that value can be traced back to a single, simple observation by one wide-awake person.

Taking the blinders off

If you've ever been to New York City, chances are you've been to Penn Station.

One particularly cold and nasty day last winter, I took the train down from Tivoli to spend a few days in the city. When I emerged from the station, I saw a long line of people waiting for taxis. 'Long' as in 50 to 75 people long.

Right across the street from Penn Station is the old Pennsylvania Hotel. There's a taxi stop there too. Only instead of the line being 50 to 75 people long, there are usually no more than 2 or 3 people waiting.

So why did so many people stand in front of Penn Station on that long, long line and wait 15 to 20 minutes in the freezing cold for a taxi when all they had to do was cross the street and hop into one?

Here are two reasons I came up with:

#1. They're not observing what's around them.

#2. They're going with the crowd. 'The crowd' is waiting, therefore waiting must be the thing to do.

Interestingly enough, as I crossed the street, I found myself entertaining doubts about my decision: "Can this be right? Can it really be this easy? After all, if all it takes to get a cab right now instead of 20 minutes from now is to cross the street, wouldn't everyone be doing it? There must be a catch. I must be missing something."

In fact, I wasn't missing anything. In a minute I was in a warm cab barreling downtown.

Two mental habits keep people from making progress - and money: 1) Not paying attention to what's in front of their noses and 2) Assuming that 'the crowd' knows what it's doing.

These two expensive mental habits are well worth breaking... and you can break them instantly if you assume that 'school' is <u>always</u> in session and it's up to <u>you</u> to extract the big lessons.

"Don't Make Me Think"

There's a book that's so well titled that you almost don't even need to read it, there's so much power on the cover: "Don't make me think." It's by web usability expert Steve Krug and even though he's not a marketer, there's a million dollars worth of marketing advice in those four words.

Here's why:

Your prospects and customers are overloaded

How many times have you gone to a web site or a store with money burning a hole in your pocket desperate to buy something you urgently needed only to give up because of all the hoops the 'sales' department requires you to jump through?

It's practically an epidemic.

Yesterday I tried to give $250 to a consumer electronics web site for a new iPod. I tried eight times before I finally gave up and went somewhere else.

Most businesses don't need to hire super-salespeople to enjoy a healthy bump up in sales. They just need to remove the obstacles.

No one has time to think

One of the biggest obstacles to closing sales is asking your customer to think.

I'm not suggesting that prospects and customers can't think, but I am saying that even if they like to think and are capable of thinking, they simply don't have the time.

This is why simple language and 'clear as glass' direction win the day in sales letters and on web pages. It's not a matter of 'speaking down' to your prospects; it's matter of making sure you've removed every potential source of confusion.

How to make the 'brave new world' work for you

A sale is a very fragile thing and confusion is a killer. Folks who teach ad writing talk about the need to grab your prospect's attention, to hold his interest, to stimulate his desire. These are all well and good and they are essential. But what's missing from most copywriting training is the utter importance of simple clarity.

Grab some friends (or strangers) who've never been to your web site or read your sales letter and sit them down in front of the computer... and watch. Then ask them what you're offering.

9 times out of 10 you'll be shocked. Freeman Godsen, once named 'The Man of the Year' by the Direct Marketing Association, used to bring his sales letters to the supermarket and pay the clerks to read them

to see if they made sense. He said it was the <u>most prof-</u><u>itable</u> research money his firm ever spent - and I believe it.

In a world where time and attention are at a premium, the marketer who makes it simple for his pro-spects and customers - simple to read the ad, simple to understand the benefits, simple to see the value, simple to place the order - will be the winner every time.

Customers...and Business
...and Wealth

There's a world of difference between a <u>business</u> and a promotion.

A business is something that makes money day after day. A promotion is an event.

Promotions are an important part of business-building, but they are <u>not</u> businesses. A lot of people, including some very famous marketing 'gurus,' misunderstand the difference.

The key distinction between a business and a promotion is a business has <u>customers</u> while a promotion has buyers. Customers are people who make it a <u>custom</u> to buy from you. In other words, they come back again and again. Mere buyers come and go.

To build a real business - not just a promotion - focus on the <u>customer building</u> process.

The wrong way to do it

Sometimes the clearest way to learn how to do something right is to observe people who get it wrong. For example:

• A now well known Internet marketing guru surprised me by describing his attitude towards customers this way: "Customers suck!"

• A world famous copywriting guru likes to wear a baseball cap to his own seminars with the words "Clients Suck" emblazoned on the front.

• A well regarded direct marketing expert jokingly confided to me that instead of providing the service he received money for, he'd actually prefer to hit his customers over the head, empty their pockets and dump their unconscious bodies in the desert. He was joking... I think.

All three individuals are superb <u>promoters</u>. When they're inspired, they can make more money in the space of a few weeks than some businesses make all year.

The truth is, you can learn a great deal from them about selling and promoting, but they're missing the big picture - and frankly, it shows in their personal and financial lives. (Many 'super salesmen' have a strange way of blowing all their money and ending up broke.)

Sales <u>and</u> customer service

The sales world is sexy. It's filled with tales of drama and daring and spectacular success stories - but it's only <u>half</u> the business story. Yes, you have to be able to get people in the door, but to have a <u>business</u>, you have to <u>keep them</u> there. Peter Drucker put it best with just eight words: "The purpose of business is to create customers."

The way to keep customers is customer service. It's a terrible term. It sounds boring and tedious and unfortunately, real customer service is so rare these days, the phrase 'customer service' is almost a bad joke. Yet the truly smart business people of the world - the people who build lasting businesses and real wealth - take customer service very seriously.

Yes, it can be exhausting to sell, run a business, and deal with customers, but ultimately dealing with customers is what it's all about. This doesn't mean that you have to personally handle every single customer issue, but as your business grows, you want to make sure that mechanisms for customer service grow along with it.

'Customer loyalty' - What do you think of when you hear that term? Most entrepreneurs think about it in terms of a customer's loyalty to their business, and how rare it is these days. Here's a way to turn that idea on its head and make a lot of money...

Instead of worrying about customers being loyal to you, how about asking how loyal you are to them?

The fact is that 'hidden' attitudes towards your customers don't stay hidden long.

Business and wealth builders go beyond clever sales promotions and think long and hard about how to serve their customers after the sale. That's where the real money gets made.

A Formula for Generating
Productive Action - Part One

In our November System Club interview, we heard the story of two guys who took a very small action (starting an online discussion board) and leveraged it into one quarter of a BILLION dollars in sales. What's the moral of the story?

Some 'gurus' might say it demonstrates the power of discussion boards and that you should start one right away. A slightly more sophisticated guru might say this was an example of the power of 'taking action.'

They'd both be missing the big picture.

From zero to $248,300,000 –
How did they do that?

'Take action!' You've probably heard that advice a million times. It's good advice, but it's incomplete. It's incomplete because it doesn't answer the million-dollar question: what kind of action.

Our November Club guests followed a very simple formula that told them exactly what to do at every stage of their business.

They might not have been consciously aware of this formula, but I can safely say it is the secret behind their success story and every success story on earth.

This formula boils down to just three seemingly simple questions that you ask yourself about anything you're working on (or not working on as the case may be.)

1. What's working?
2. What's missing?
3. What's next?

I love this formula because it's so simple, it focuses your mind on the right things, and it automatically generates <u>productive</u> actions.

'What's working?' - Our November guests started a business facing a challenge as huge as Mt. Everest. They were inexperienced, under-funded, and outgunned by people with 10,000 times more resources than they had. So what did they do? They scanned the landscape to find something that was working. In their case, a small group of people (just 40) were spontaneously posting to a discussion board about their proposed product. That became their starting point.

'What's missing?' - The discussion board situation was missing some things. First, it wasn't their board so they had limited control over what they could do with it. Second, the then-hot discussion was, like all discussions, eventually going to lose steam if they didn't add more fuel to the fire.

'What's next?' - Once you've discovered something that's working and catalogued the things that are missing from it that can make it better and more powerful, your next steps become blazingly obvious.

In the case of our November Club meeting guests, they started their <u>own</u> board and then started on a program of regularly throwing another log on the fire to keep the discussion going and growing.... and the rest is history.

This formula stimulates <u>real</u> positive thinking. More about it next week. Meanwhile, try it out.

A Formula for Generating
<u>Productive</u> Action - Part Two

The formula:

1. What's working?
2. What's missing?
3. What's next?

These six simple words offer an incomparable tool for solving problems, uncovering new opportunities, and keeping your life and business on track. This week, let's focus on the first part of the formula.

"What's working?"

I recently read a fascinating story about a young American stock trader who noticed an impending event that was going to cause a major, one-day movement in stock prices. He sold the idea to his boss and his firm rolled the dice on it. The result? He was right and his firm made $50 million in one day. He became a hero.

This fellow spent the next year looking for his next 'big hit' and found himself drilling one 'dry well' after another. After a while, he despaired that he'd never come up with another blockbuster trading idea again. Then a colleague - in a completely offhanded remark - said 'why don't you try that thing that worked so well for you last year?'

Sure enough, a search of the news revealed that the one-day anomaly that had worked so well for him in one market (Hong Kong), was about to repeat itself in another market (Japan). Now, having the benefit of the experience of having done it once successfully, his firm took an even bigger position - and the trader negotiated a much better cut for himself. The result? He was right and the firm made $500 million in one day - and he got a 15% performance bonus...$75 million dollars. Not bad for a day's work.

Obviously, this is an extreme example of the value of paying attention to - and <u>remembering</u> - 'what's working?' but opportunities to profit from <u>what's working</u> come up all the time in business and life.

Overcoming the big blind spot

I don't know why this is so, but it seems that virtually everyone - including me - has a strong tendency to overlook and undervalue things that are going well, working naturally and progressing smoothly.

For example, when we face challenges, we often get very creative about how we imagine the challenge (we make it bigger and more formidable than it really is). At the same time, we get very <u>uncreative</u> about remembering and properly valuing all the resources we <u>already</u> possess that can help us overcome it.

The quick solution to many challenges is to search out, catalog and keep the things that are working for you at the forefront of your mind. The answer you're seeking may be in your own experience, or in the mind of a person you have easy access to, or someone in his or her network.

128

Another example of the blind spot is when looking for business opportunities we tend to look for the new, the exotic, the far away instead of the things we already know well and are close at hand.

Contrast this with Sam Walton, founder of Wal-Mart who looked around, saw a need for a good department store in the rural town that he lived in and started one. The first store worked so well, he decided to try another one. His biggest goal was to own two stores; that he decided would be real success. Instead of stopping there, he paid attention to the things that were working - and he worked them.

What's already working in your life and business? How can you do more of it?

A Formula for Generating
Productive Action - Part Three

The formula:
1. What's working?
2. What's missing?
3. What's next?

The reason I got involved in Internet marketing so early was because I saw that powerful <u>external</u> forces - cheaper PCs, faster modems, and better online interfaces - were coming together and that tens of thousands of people had <u>already</u> spontaneously made the online world a daily part of their lives.

I reasoned that anyone who established themselves early on as a credible expert on online marketing was going to be in the proverbial 'catbird seat' (i.e. a prominent place to which business flows effortlessly.)

Bottom line: Success comes from <u>harnessing</u>, not creating social forces. There's quite a bit of creative leeway in exactly <u>how</u> you harness a given force, but behind <u>every</u> success story there's always an underlying force that made the success possible in the first place.

Instant improvement

The great copywriter Eugene Schwartz called his mail order publishing company, INSTANT IMPROVEMENT. There's a lifetime of hard won insight and experience behind that name.

Here's why:

People trade dollars for stuff, for one reason and one reason only: to improve their situation. Even when they do crazy stuff with their money, their underlying - if sometimes misguided - motivation is always to make their current situation better...because they perceive there is something missing from it.

Viewed from this angle, business success is not so much about creating new products and then heroically bringing them to market, as it is finding <u>existing</u> markets that are missing something.

If you live in a big urban area, you've probably seen the phenomenon of the super successful, high end, non-chain convenience store owned and operated by first generation immigrants from Asia. When I lived in San Francisco, I had the opportunity to carefully track the development of one of these stores over a period of years.

At first, the store was practically empty. I wondered if they were going to make it. Then bit by bit, it filled up and got more and more organized until finally, when I moved back east, the place was a showcase.

How did they do it? Simple. They asked every customer what they thought the store should carry - what's missing? - and when enough people mentioned the same thing, they stocked it. In short, their method of marketing and business development was to pay careful attention to what was missing.

You can also apply the 'what's missing?' method to problem solving in your own business. Clearly there are things that are already working well in every business. Focus on them. Expand on them. Consciously grow them. But what about the things that aren't working so well?

The first question to ask about something that isn't working is "Do I need to be doing this thing in the first place?" If you don't, the easiest way to solve the problem is to stop doing the thing at all.

But if it is something you need or want to do, the next step is to sit down and make a list of what's missing from the situation and then develop a plan to go out and get it. This is an infinitely more productive thing than focusing on and feeling overwhelmed by the problem. All problems seem to boil down to either excess or deficiency. Problems of excess are solved by elimination, problems of deficiency by adding the missing pieces.

What's Next?

I recently discovered that the concept of 'brainstorming' - asking questions to stimulate new business ideas - was first championed by a guy named Alex Osborn. His book "Applied Imagination" was a best seller in 1953.

Osborn introduced the idea - one I firmly believe in by the way - that breakthroughs are not the product of rare 'geniuses,' but are a natural outcome of processes that everyone can learn, use, and profit from.

So onwards to the last part of our three-question process for generating productive action.

"What's next?" - the third and final stage of the formula - moves your mind along in an orderly process from observation ("What's working?") and speculation ("What's missing?") to action. It's the easiest part of the process after you've completed the previous two steps.

Not an idle question

To give you a concrete example of how to apply this formula in real life, here's how I used it to help evolve the System.

<u>What's working</u> was offering quality and making high level <u>education</u> the first and foremost purpose of the System.

<u>What's missing</u> was twofold: 1) there was no easy way for beginners to get 'up to speed', 2) There was no way, other than the System Club, for experienced Internet marketers to take their game to the next level.

With what's working and missing nailed down, "What's next?" was pretty easy and for me, it looked like this:

1) <u>Smart Beginners</u>, a System-level home study course for beginners so they can master the building block ABCs of Internet marketing, <u>before</u> they come to a System training.

2) <u>System Intensives</u>, advanced, limited-enrollment trainings for pros and people aspiring to become pros to get into the nitty-gritty depth and intricacies of key Internet marketing specialties that simply can't be dealt with in mass meeting type seminars.

A new vision

These new initiatives freed up the System seminar to become a true graduate alumni conference where the knowledge base of attendees is sky high and the focus is on what's new and where the Internet is headed, not on trying to educate folks from scratch.

Values and Vision in Business and Life

"Cowardice asks the question, 'Is it safe?'

Expediency asks the question, 'Is it politic?'

Vanity asks the question, 'Is it popular?'

But conscience asks the question, 'Is it right?'

And there comes a time when one must take a position that is neither safe, nor politic, nor popular, but one must take it because one's conscience tells one that it is right."

- Martin Luther King

I'd like to recommend a book to you called "Built to Last: Successful Habits of Visionary Companies" by Jim Collins and Jerry Porras. It was originally published in 1994, has gone through forty printings since, been translated into thirteen languages and has topped best seller lists in the US, Canada, Japan, South America and Europe...a successful info product to say the least.

Though the book is primarily a study of big companies, there's a lot in it for scrappy entrepreneurs. Like all good writers, researchers and teachers, Collins and Porras do a great job of demolishing myths and one of the ones they do a number on is the idea that the greatest business success goes to people who put profits above all else.

Instead of basing their findings on 'overnight success' stories, the two authors studied businesses that have survived and thrived for decades - in some cases over 100 years - and that have substantially outperformed their competitors financially. Their conclusion: Hyper-aggressive, profits-before-honor companies do make money, sometimes lots of money, but at the end of the day they end up eating the dust of companies with values.

Here's a fascinating quote from one of the CEO's interviewed for the book:

"It may take us longer to get established in a new culture, especially if we have difficulty finding people who fit with our value system. Take China and Russia, for example, where you'll find rampant corruption and dishonesty. So, we move more slowly, and grow only as fast as we can find people who will uphold our standards. And we're willing to forgo business opportunities that would force us to abandon our principles.

We're still in business after 100 years, doubling in size every six or seven years, when most of our competitors from fifty years ago don't even exist any more. Why? Because of the discipline to not compromise our standards for the sake of expediency. In everything we do, we take the long view. Always."

Visionary companies - as Collins and Porras call them - tend to ask themselves 'weird' questions. Instead of asking 'How well am I doing?' they ask 'How can I do, what I'm already doing well, even better?' Instead of asking themselves 'How can I make myself rich?' they ask 'How can I make myself rich and make the world around me a better place?

From the authors' note: "Why on earth would you settle for creating something mediocre that does little more than make money, when you can create something outstanding that makes a lasting contribution as well?"

Warning: Genius at Work

The dictionary tells us a genius is 'a person of extraordinary intellect and talent.' The news media and our schools tell us that geniuses are <u>born</u> that way and are made of different (better) stuff than the rest of us.

I could not disagree more.

To paraphrase a line from the movie FOREST GUMP: "Genius is as genius <u>does</u>."

I do believe in inborn talent. I also believe in the near magical powers of enthusiasm and passion, but I also believe that there is no such thing as genius. It's a myth, a fairy tale, make believe. As a piece of 'showmanship' it's a good strategy for selling, but as a way of describing the way the world really works, it's a total flop.

The awesome power behind a
four letter word

I've had the opportunity to meet and spend extended time with several people that the world at large considers geniuses (in the fields of music and business.) I've also read in depth about the lives of geniuses and talked with people who've worked with them. (Just the other night I had dinner with a neighbor who worked for ten years with the painter Robert Rauschenberg who is possibly the world's most respected living artist.)

I can tell you from these experiences, and my friend will back it up, that 'geniuses', no matter how far out they seem, really do put their pants on one leg at a time. In fact, unless you actually see a genius at his or her <u>work</u>, you could very easily overlook them.

And that, of course, is the four letter word that makes all the difference: <u>work</u>.

But work alone obviously isn't enough. Lots of people work and many people work very hard without producing genius results. So what's the missing ingredient? Some people say it's talent, but I say they're wrong. Talent is nothing more than a raw material and an inert one at that.

The real work

I'm opening up a topic here that can't be adequately covered in one page or even one hundred pages, but I can give you something to chew on: Every 'genius' I've ever met or worked with is <u>profoundly</u> involved in a never-ending program of creative self-education. Yes, they work hard. That's a given, but they also consistently work on expanding themselves...on stretching.

Jim Rohn, one of the great practical philosophers of our time, puts it this way: "If you work hard at your job, you'll make a living. If you work hard on yourself, you'll make a fortune."

How do you 'work on yourself?' If you don't know how, you're in good company because this is certainly not a subject taught in school or on the job or in most families - and yet, it is the single most important topic for people who are pursuing achievement.

A highly regarded artist and dancer - a woman with the intriguing name of Twyla Tharp - came out with a book two years ago called "The Creative Habit: Learn It and Use It for Life." A smart marketer could easily package the gold in her book into a $5,000 seminar.

You can get it now at Amazon for all of $16.50. It's packed with immediately practical ideas on how to 'stretch' your potential into places you may never have dreamed possible. Good reading for these long, cold winter nights.

If you've been a System Club member for a while, you know who Richard Koch is. If you haven't and Richard's work is new to you, then you're in for a treat... and a life changing one at that.

You've probably heard of the 80/20 principle. It's discussed a lot in sales circles. "20% of a sales force is responsible for 80% of the sales." "20% of your customers are responsible for 80% of your profits." And so on.

So the 80/20 Principle is probably not news to you.

What is new is that Richard took this idea - one of the most researched, tested, and verified principles in the social sciences - and discovered dozens of practical ways to use it and profit.

As a result, while a lot of us run around from dawn 'til dusk, working ourselves too hard and under too much stress, Richard lives a life of leisure in one of his three homes (London, Cape Town, the south of Spain) making millions on businesses that he takes over, rehabs and sells for enormous profits.

Some of his 'hits' include Filfax (the personal organizer) and Plymouth (a premium gin brand.) We're not talking about eBooks here, but significant multi-million dollar companies that have made him, and continue to make him, a very wealthy man. His current project, Betfair, the world's leading betting exchange is on track to make him a high eight and possible nine figure profit.

How does he achieve these extraordinary results? He says his secret is the 80/20 Principle.

"Modern life is a mistake"

Koch has come out with a popularly written book that's an improvement on his original classic "The 80/20 Principle" which he calls "Living the 80/20 Way."

The book starts with a succinct and dramatic summary of the principle: "The 80/20 Way enables anyone to get extraordinary results without extraordinary effort."

That's quite a claim, especially when you break it down. The 'Way' will work for anyone. It will produce not just results, but extraordinary results. Those who use the 'Way' achieve their extraordinary results without extraordinary effort.

The difference between Koch and others who make similar claims is that he has a method based on science, he has proved his method over and over again in the hardball world of venture capitalism, and in his latest book, he offers a step-by-step system for teaching yourself to follow the 80/20 way.

Do you think that more is better and greater efforts bring greater results? If you do, then you're in step with modern times, but Koch says you're out of step with the proven, natural laws of success.

Greater achievement, less effort, more happiness. Koch has it down better than anyone else I've ever heard of.

When to 'Break the Rules'
Part One

When you're first learning how to do something, Step One is to follow the rules, also known by the less authoritative phrase 'master the fundamentals.'

There's a great paradox in this because very often, spectacular success comes from NOT following the rules.

So which is it? Follow the rules or break the rules?

(By the way, when I talk about 'breaking the rules,' I'm not talking about breaking laws, temporal or moral. I'm talking about going 'outside the box' of approved technique.)

Here's a good rule of thumb for dealing with this paradox:

When you're a student, follow the rules slavishly. Pick your teacher well of course, but once you've chosen him or her, do exactly as they tell you.

Good teachers will have a rock solid foundation in the fundamentals of their craft, whatever it may be... and because they know how important the fundamentals are to your success, they will drill you in them over and over without any concern as to whether you find the experience 'entertaining' or not.

As a young teenager, I had a basketball coach who had been a High School All-American. In his day, he had gone head-to-head with Kareem Abdul Jabar (then known as Lew Alcindor of Power Memorial High School, who at 7 feet plus was one of the most talented and accomplished basketball players who ever lived.)

My coach Mr. Summinski - and thirty plus years later I still wouldn't dream of calling him anything else - wasn't the tallest, the fastest or slickest player on the court. He knew that the only way he could succeed was to be the most solid and he drilled (actually beat) that into us too.

The result is that, after one year in his hands, our team went from being truly pathetic (we lost one of our first games by over 100 points) to being able to go head-to-head with teams from Newark and East Orange and, even if we didn't always win, we were always in the game.

(If you're not from NJ, just be aware that no one fools around on a basketball court in those cities and comes out alive. For example, getting an 'accidental' forearm across the nose while going up for a rebound was not an uncommon event. If your skills weren't rock solid, the game could be over practically before it began.)

What 'secret' techniques did Mr. Summinski teach to effect such an amazing transformation over us? Passing, dribbling, lay-ups, foul shots and rebounding. Over and over and over again.

Mr. Summinksi didn't care whether he entertained us. He didn't care whether we liked him or not. But he did care that we learned the skills he was entrusted to teach us - and he succeeded massively.

I think I've made the case for the power of following the rules. When does it make sense to break them?

The answer comes in two parts...

1. Don't even think about breaking the rules until you've mastered them inside and out.

My grammar school basketball team wasn't the most talented on the court, but we consistently ate the lunch of 'better' teams that lacked our relentlessly disciplined, fundamentals-based approach to the game.

2. Once you've mastered the rules, there is one situation I can think of where breaking the rules not only makes sense, but can lead to extraordinary success.

When to 'Break the Rules'
Part Two

An important part of learning is following the rules, but an important part of making <u>real</u> progress is learning when to break them. So when does it make sense to 'break the rules.'

The creation of Disneyland is a classic case of breaking the rules.

Before Disney, amusement parks were temporary, traveling affairs. Carnival operators would arrive in a town, pay off the local police, rip the townspeople off blind, and then head to the next town before they were lynched.

Before Disney that was the model for "doing it right."

Disney had a better idea - so he broke all the rules

Disney asked: "What about building a <u>permanent</u> amusement park that provides a clean and safe place where families could go together to enjoy themselves without being treated like 'marks' and scammed?

A place so well managed and so elaborately put together and in such a fascinating manner that families would travel to <u>it</u> instead of the other way around."

In the 1950s when Disney was trying to raise the money for his idea, it seemed crazy and farfetched. Today, even with all the problems at the top, the Disney Empire is a juggernaut and has become the most visited tourist destination on earth.

Sell one thing at a time

This February I'm putting on THREE different seminars in Miami. This is a major violation of the marketing law, which, quite rightly, states "Sell one thing at a time."

I can confirm it is hard to launch and promote three different seminar products at the same time and I'm not sure that I'll ever do it again, but I'm glad I did it, and if I had to do it over again I would. Here's why:

Each one of these (sold out) seminars represents an urgent MISSION to me.

First, there was no place people could go to learn to improve their skills as Internet marketing consultants. Second, there was no place to go to learn how to sell physical products online. Third, while there's some good copywriting material circulating on the Internet, there's a lot of stuff out there that's so bad it's positively dangerous.

To me this was crazy state of affairs and once the System community got big enough to support specialized trainings like the ones we're doing this month, I wanted to 'break the ice' and get the ball rolling on these trainings without any unnecessary delay.

So when do you break the rules? When the rules create a negative effect or when your mission says "It needs to happen now. The rules be damned."

Numbers - Real,
Make-Believe and Silly

Numbers are the fuel that runs business. They let you know when you're on track and when you're off track. They highlight areas of opportunity - and potential black holes. They can even inspire and motivate.

But numbers can cripple too, or at the very least they can distract you and rob you of your enjoyment of your business. 'Enjoyment' is a <u>crucial</u> aspect of business-building because if, at the end of the day, the process is not satisfying, you'll never put in the work required to make it really work.

Make-believe numbers

Enron...

For years, people in the legitimate energy industry were scratching their heads over Enron's numbers. "How are they doing that? Why can't <u>we</u> do that?" I'm sure Enron's 'success' agitated many inferiority complexes and inspired a lot of boardroom screaming matches.

Then Enron's chief executives were taken away in handcuffs. They were lying about their numbers.

We've got a bit of that in the Internet marketing guru world too.

It can range from things as simple as inflating the number of people on a tele-seminar to claiming sales figures and visitor numbers that bear no relation to reality.

Why do they do it? It's easy. They want sales <u>now</u> and they don't care how they get them. Rather than <u>earn</u> a reputation by making real contributions and real accomplishments, they choose to steal one instead.

Silly numbers hurt too

You've seen the formula: "I made X dollars in just one (day, week, month!!!)"

I stay away from this myself. I report success stories in terms of <u>repeating</u> monthly or annual revenue, not one-time, 'special circumstance' sales spikes. Personally, I am <u>far</u> more impressed by someone who is regularly bringing in $5,000 a month than someone who <u>once</u> made $50,000 in a day. The $5,000 a month person has a solid base to build on. The '$50,000 in a day' windfall guy may or may not be able to repeat it.

Sure, windfalls and huge sales spikes are 'cool.' We should all work towards them and enjoy them fully when they take place, but <u>real</u> business is not a fireworks display. Big pay 'days' are invariably the result of lots of behind-the-scenes work, taking care of business day in and day out, for months and years on end.

I've said before that there is no Great Bean Counter in the sky who decides who can and who cannot make money and how much everyone is 'allowed' to make.

Money comes from 'wiring.' It's a matter of putting attractive offers in front of receptive buyers and then delivering on your promises. How to make that happen is really the <u>only</u> thing we should think about. While we can learn much from the success of others, it's NOT their reported numbers that is instructive, it's the <u>reality</u> of what it took to generate those numbers.

Look <u>behind</u> the curtain. Don't get dazzled by the stage show.

Take pride and satisfaction in your <u>consistent</u> daily efforts and ignore silly numbers. The <u>real</u> numbers you'll generate by building a real business will be far more interesting and satisfying - and maybe even bigger too.

What Gardeners Know

A huge portion of the world's food is still grown in gardens and when push comes to shove, as in Russia during the financial collapse a few years back or in the US and elsewhere during World War II, gardeners are the back up force that puts food on the table in times of trouble.

Not only that, but virtually every worthwhile advance in agriculture over the last several thousand years started in someone's garden, not in an agri-business laboratory or corporation-owned farm.

One of the great pleasures of living in Tivoli is that after twenty years of living in cities (roughly ten in New York and ten in San Francisco), Bettina and I can finally have a real garden. Bettina's much more diligent about hers than I am of mine (you should see it, it's beautiful), but I make sure that every year I put something in the ground.

What gardening taught me about business building

1. It's all about the soil.

When you think about it, plants are incredibly complex. One tiny seed contains enough instructions in it to take a plant through several dramatic changes: from seedling to rapid growth and leaf development, to flowering, to fruiting and finally seeding. And the whole show runs on just a handful of elements: sun, water, temperature, various gases and soil - and that's it.

The one thing the gardener has total control over is soil. All other things being equal, good soil equals success. Poor soil equals a tough time and probably failure.

It's the same thing in marketing. The first - and last - element in successful marketing is market selection. Just as you can't grow plants on rock or in sand, you can't reasonably expect to build a successful business without a good sized, hungry, <u>reachable</u> market. Every single one of those elements must be in place.

2. Conditions determine what you can grow.

You may <u>want</u> to grow sugar cane in New England, but the fact is that that particular plant just isn't suited to that environment. Rather than trying to force something to grow in a climate that's wrong for it, why not figure out what will grow easily and naturally in a particular setting?

Business conditions come and go. What's a gold mine today may become a ghost town tomorrow. A huge portion of 'success' comes simply from being in the right market at the right time with the right stuff. Swimming upstream, while heroic, is generally not good business.

3. When you do things right, nature does the real work.

In gardening there is a lot of work: preparing the soil, choosing the right seeds, regular watering and so on, but in reality the vast majority of the work is done for you. You don't really 'grow' the plants. They grow themselves. The gardener's art is to orchestrate congenial surroundings so that the plants can do their thing with as few obstacles as possible.

Most businesses have well functioning 'Sales Prevention' Departments and 'Employee De-motivation' Programs. You can liken these aberrations to weeds. They grow outside of our awareness, starting small and then - if neglected - growing relentlessly until they threaten to choke the life out of our business.

Most obstacles in business are either self-inflicted or they're the result of simply not paying attention. Good gardeners are in the garden most every day, removing things that don't belong and finding ways, large and small, to make it easier for the natural forces at work. And that's what smart business owners do too. They're among their customers daily, listening, learning, and experimenting with new ways to serve them.

About Liquidity

"There are few things more unbalancing to the mind than the act of suddenly winning or losing large sums of money." - Henry Howard Harper, The Psychology of Speculation

One of the best educations I ever got was the time I spent working on Wall Street. It was the roaring 80s and the market seemed invulnerable. It wasn't and I was right there when the whole thing melted down. It made an impression on me.

Punch bowls, bubbles, and musical chairs

Most of the time, I focus on the particulars of running an Internet business and using the Internet to boost existing businesses. Today, I'd like to talk a little bit about money in the broader sense.

First my biases. I am extremely conservative financially. I am very positive about my ability to make money, but I am also very realistic about the vagaries of life.

The reality - as I see it - is that we are living in a period of extraordinary opportunity, especially for folks who know how to use the Internet to find and serve customers. One of the reasons I've poured so much effort into teaching in the last few years is, quite literally:

"Now's the time." Now is the time to rack up cash - but keep in mind, it won't always be this way.

We are currently experiencing a period of financial liquidity unlike anything ever seen before in the history of this country. Liquidity in this context simply means: There is a ton of money around right now. A TON.

Yes, we are good marketers and yes, we are good business people and yes, we work hard and yes, we have been clever, but we're also profiting from the fact that the Central Banks of the world, especially our own, have been printing money like there is no tomorrow.

Well, there will be a tomorrow. There always is. At some point, the punch bowl will be taken away and the party will be over (at least until the next time.) If you're old enough to have seen such a time, or you've read some history, you already know it's not fun for the un-prepared. So what do you do to prepare?

Suggestions for a happy landing

1. By all means, enjoy the party - especially the part that involves you aggressively making and salting away cash.

2. But don't assume the entire reason you're doing well is because you are: a) a financial genius or b) graced by God. The liquidity explosion has helped us all a lot by putting easy money in large quantities into our customers' pockets.

3. Don't be in a mad race to jack up your lifestyle to keep pace with your rising income. I'm not saying

live in a hut and wear a burlap sack, but be ruthless about living like a normal person, not a player on a roll. The best things in life really <u>are</u> free, something frighteningly easy to forget when you're on a spending spree.

4. Don't make big long term bets on things that depend on: 1) cheap oil and 2) consumers having easy money coming out of their ears. I don't have a crystal ball, but history says neither of these conditions are permanent.

5. Think musical chairs. In short, don't be the guy who has so overextended himself on lifestyle enhancements and bubble investments that when the music stops, you're one of the ones left without a chair.

You know the story of the Grasshopper and the Ant. And the Seven Years of Plenty and the Seven Years of Famine. There's a reason those stories have been around for a long, long time. Let's prosper together <u>throughout</u> the ups and downs of the business cycle, not just on one sunny turn of the wheel. History shows that people with perspective end up being the biggest winners in the money game.

Note: this article was originally published July, 2005.

The entrepreneurial world is not an easy one to crack.

While there's been a recent proliferation of trainings (some good, some not so good), entrepreneurs, by definition have to be self-starters. Ultimately, every entrepreneur has to find his or her own way. It ain't easy - but it sure is rewarding.

I subscribe to a lot of entrepreneurial newsletters in all kinds of fields from ranching to foreign exchange trading to real estate. Being exposed to a variety of other people's experiences (OPE) helps keep my mind limber.

One of my favorite newsletters is by a guy named Jack Miller, the pioneer of creative real estate training who is still teaching and going strong in his 80s.

Jack came up with many of the concepts that are now trumpeted on TV infomercials. Instead of going 'show biz', he's chosen to focus on creating consistently great, high level content for a select group of discriminating students - and he's done very well for himself.

Recently, Jack published his list of the things he is grateful for.

Whether you've already made the transition to being an entrepreneur or are still working towards it, take a look at Jack's thoughtful list and you'll quickly be reminded of what we are working for and what a great deal we as entrepreneurs have - even if sometimes it can be a tough and lonely road.

"What I'm thankful for" by Jack Miller

- I am healthy, productive and happy
- I'm surrounded by family and friends who support what I do
- I live and work in a lovely place that I selected myself
- I don't have to commute to work at all. No rush-hour traffic.
- I get to wear (or not wear) anything I like all day long.
- My pay is based solely on how long and productively I want to work
- I get to start work as early as I want, and to work at late as I want
- I can take vacations where and when I want without asking permission
- I have no boss to make me waste my time and do stupid things
- I get to make all the decisions regarding my financial security and that of my family
- I am free to take responsibility for all my activities, good and bad
- I can do what I do in any place in America and in many foreign lands

• I am able to make more than most of the people in the world

• Because I work for myself, my company won't be merged

• I don't have to worry about being laid-off, down-sized or fired

• My retirement plan is within my control

As entrepreneurs, we enjoy many things, large and small, that the average person - even someone with a 'great job' - can't even imagine.

Stay the course. It <u>is</u> worth it.

Two Books about Success

If you want to read a somewhat strange, but true story about: 1) the Internet as a community-building engine, 2) the power of harnessing deeply felt drives, and 3) the dynamics of 'guru-dom,' check out the book "The Game" by Neil Strauss.

This is not a 'how-to' marketing book. In fact, in many ways it is a 'how-not-to' book. The protagonists achieved their 'dreams,' became rock star famous among their followers, made mountains of money – and then proceeded to make themselves and everyone around them miserable.

This story is not as uncommon as you think. Many of you may have grabbed hold of the brass ring and discovered what Johnny Carson discovered and so eloquently described late into his hyper-successful career: "The road to success is always under construction." Note the word always.

The hazards of being a guru

Being a guru is a great thing from a marketing point of view. The reason why is simple: People overwhelmingly prefer to buy from gurus. Less than 1 person out of 100 (maybe it's less than 1 out of 10,000) will invest the time, expense and mental energy it takes to seek out and evaluate claims in the search of real expertise.

In contrast, it's infinitely easier for people to press the 'Order' button to buy from 'The Big Name' even if the big name is just an empty headed poser.

That's the way it is, so it makes sense for us to do everything we can to position ourselves in our niches as The Guru.

There's just one catch – and no one ever talks about this. Becoming a guru comes with real hazards.

Ideally, guru-dom is like a special suit of clothes you put on for business and then take off at the end of the day. Where people run into trouble is when they start believing their own PR. It's the surest way to 'snatch defeat from the jaws of victory.' I see this every day in the business world and Strauss chronicles the downward process vividly in his book.

Can you be 'successful' and miserable?

Absolutely. And that's where the second book comes in. It's long been one of my favorite business books. It can be a bit kooky in places, but when it's on, it's 10,000% on the money. It's called "The Trick to Money is Having Some" by Stuart Wilde and as I read "The Game" bits and pieces of Wilde's wisdom bubbled up.

I'm paraphrasing, but here's the takeaway lesson from Wilde's very astute analysis of business and financial success: "Success is not what you have, it's how you feel about what you have."

When I first read this book, I was struggling – really struggling – financially and I thought Wilde was full of hot air and off the point. Now having been back and forth on both sides of the divide, I realize he hit the nail on the head perfectly.

The mechanics of making money is very straightforward. It's a lot like going to trade school and learning how to be a plumber. Connect the pipes the right way and the money flows. It's a complete impartial, non-mystical process.

The real challenge of the game is disciplining yourself - and it is a discipline - to enjoy the process and enjoy where you're at wherever that may be. This is, in fact, the most intensely practical - and sustainable – foundation for creating lasting success in any endeavor.

There are two ways that wealth is created. Just two.

The first way is celebrated in movies, novels, and in 'get rich quick' sales letters. The second method is nowhere near as glamorous, but it's infinitely more certain.

Wealth Creation Method #1 is what I call The Grand Slam.

One of the most famous examples of The Grand Slam is the story of how currency speculator George Soros made a huge and seemingly risky bet against the British Pound and raked one billion dollars off the table in a single day's worth of trading. Even though that trade took place two decades ago and represents only a small portion of the wealth he's created, that's the story everyone talks about when they talk about the success of George Soros.

Grand slams defined

The key to this story, and all the others like it, is overnight riches coming from one stunningly brilliant and gutsy move. It makes for exciting ad copy, but it's a terrible way to conceive a business.

Since it's World Series time, let me use a baseball analogy to explain why.

In baseball, there's a thing called a 'grand slam.' That's when there's a player on every base and the batter hits a home run bringing in FOUR runs with a single swing of the bat. A grand slam is always a dramatic event because they're so rare and scoring four points at one bat, let alone in one inning, is enough to instantly change the course of a game.

The fact is grand slams happen. Perfect games happen too. And these things become the stuff of legend, but they are horrible foundations to build a baseball strategy on – or a business strategy.

How wealth is <u>really</u> created

We all like excitement and we all want to be part of something that's larger than life, but real money-making is a quiet, modest process that has more to do with doing many unglamorous things day in and day out well than it does with hitting grand slam home runs. Success in baseball is this way too.

In order for a grand slam to even be possible, let alone meaningful, a whole lot of little things have to be done right.

First of all, the team's defense has to be good enough that it's not more than four runs behind. If your defense has been sloppy and you're down by 10, a grand slam even in the bottom of the ninth is just so much 'sound and fury.'

Second, the team's batters have to have their act

together well enough for three of them to get and stay on base in a single inning, and the 'hero' of the story has had to stay alive in the majors long enough to find himself at bat in a situation where a grand slam is possible.

This means that he's been skillful in thousands of lesser occasions: catching fly balls, not swinging at pitches out of the strike zone, and getting to first base at least two or three times for every 10 times he's been at bat.

You can't control the dramatic grand slams in business or in baseball. Situations arise. You see the potential and you act. Fate smiles. But you can hit real Grand Slams every day. It's called showing up, executing well on the things that matter no matter how large or small, and moving your enterprise one more step forward at a time. A day like that is worth a high five and when you string enough of them together, the dramatic grand slams will come too.

Review: "Power vs. Force"

A year ago, I attended a workshop on interpersonal communications skills in New York City. The only thing that really 'stuck' from it was a presentation by an unadvertised guest speaker.

This fellow arrived in a wheelchair. He had spent his entire life in one. Born with a rare genetic ailment, he was the size of a seven year old and had bones that were so fragile that something as minor as rolling over in bed the wrong way or sneezing could break one.

Writing this, I shudder just imagining the hardships of a life like his...and yet, the speaker didn't look at his life as a horror. Quite the contrary.

In spite of staggering limitations, he created success for himself professionally, financially, socially, and emotionally. He was clearly a very happy man.

He shared his secret – but I blew it off

Just being around someone like this is intensely inspiring – and it makes you think. One question that comes to mind right away is "What source is this guy drawing on? And how can I tap into it too?"

The speaker mentioned a book that he personally found helpful and illuminating and recommended it. When I went to Amazon, I saw a bunch of negative reviews ('oversimplified' 'nothing new') Even the organizer of the workshop disqualified it a bit saying it was a 'little out there.' I passed on it. So many books, so little time.

To make a long story short, I was in a bookstore last week and finally saw the book in the flesh. I picked it up and put it down. Then picked it up and put it down. (It's amazing how powerful a few negative comments can be.) Then I noticed the book had testimonials from both Sam Walton, founder of Wal-Mart, and Mother Theresa. "That's got to be a first," I thought. "If nothing else, I want to learn about a guy who can get testimonials like that!"

What's your business based on?

A lot of marketing education today focuses exclusively on technique. I call this the 'vending machine school' of business development. Entrepreneurs are told: "Put this in, push these buttons, pull this lever and success will come out." Certain aspects of direct marketing, especially Internet marketing, reinforce this point of view. And it's not entirely inaccurate. There are some techniques that work exponentially better than other techniques and they're well worth learning.

But there are other important dimensions to marketing that can't be strictly attributed to technique.

For example, the legendary direct mail wizard Dick Benson pointed out that the single best 'technique' to get people to buy a second time is to make sure the first product you sell them is excellent. Our July System

Club guest Emanuel Rosen talked about designing products that are such a 'good fit' for your marketplace that customers voluntarily help you sell them ('buzz marketing.') Our June guests, the Ginsu guys, told the story of how they used 60 seconds of celluloid to transform one of the most boring product categories in the world – kitchen knives – into a brand so powerful it's still on everyone's lips two decades after the last time the ad ran.

Sometimes in business 1 + 1 = 4 or even 94. Why? Sometimes individuals with seemingly overwhelming obstacles create lives of remarkable accomplishment and contentment. How? Clearly, there is no shortage of theories about this topic. In some ways the book "Power vs. Force" is nothing new. It is simple and parts of it are 'out there,' but it hit me like a ton of bricks (in a good way). Check it out. Highest recommendation.

Beyond
Business

Remember to Live Too

The System is about working and making money via marketing in general and the Internet in particular.

But remember 'all work and no play make Jack a dull boy.'

There's no way of getting around the necessity of hard work to survive and thrive as an entrepreneur, but clearly work is a means to an end, not the end itself.

It's easy to forget that. I know I often do.

While most of the world needs a cattle prod to get going, the entrepreneur has a different problem: to know when to stop, to take a break, to breathe...

Here's an eloquent reminder of what life is really all about. I read it at the end of the Info Marketing Institute in Orlando last winter. It's the kind of wisdom that will help keep you on track in good times and bad.

It's also as good a diagnostic test for the 'life well lived' as any I know:

"To laugh often and much,

To win the respect of intelligent people and the affection of children,

To earn the appreciation of honest critics and endure the betrayal of false friends,

To appreciate beauty,

To find the best in others,

To leave the world a bit better, whether by a healthy child, a garden patch, or a redeemed social condition,

To know even one life has breathed easier because you have lived.

This is to have succeeded! "

-Ralph Waldo Emerson

Note: Lest you think Emerson was an impractical man, he was an apple farmer, a difficult profession then and now which requires a lot of attention to detail.

Emerson's most famous student, Henry David Thoreau, famous for 'Walden Pond' and 'Civil Disobedience', was a civil engineer who perfected the process for manufacturing graphite pencils. This made his family business the biggest pencil manufacturer in the US in the era before word processors, typewriters and ball-point pens.

Birthday Thoughts

Today is my 45th birthday and I'm going to celebrate it by doing one of the things I love the most, writing about the glories of the Internet.

You may not learn how to make more money from this particular letter, but it may give you a new perspective on the medium we spend so much time of our time immersed in.

The Internet...a shining light

If you pay close attention to what's going on in the world and you care - and I do both - sometimes life can be a bit discouraging.

Money making is important, of course. It's the focus of our work together, but as Henry David Thoreau once said: "What is the use of a house if you don't have a tolerable planet to put it on?"

Every time a new medium has come along, enthusiasts are sure it will change the world. Believe it or not, none other than Herbert Hoover was once quoted as saying that he thought that radio was going to bring about universal peace and understanding.

It didn't quite work that way. In fact, just a few decades later, broadcasting became the backbone for the propaganda machines of some of the most vicious regimes the world has ever known.

The Internet is different

The Internet inspired great hopes in its early days too... but the Internet is different - it <u>delivered</u>.

No, the Internet is not going to bring about universal world peace and prosperity.

But the Internet does something almost as remarkable. It's democratizing knowledge <u>and</u> it's provided the means for an unprecedented explosion in self-publishing.

The news media doesn't talk about this - for obvious reasons - but the fact is most intelligent people have liberated themselves from 100% dependence on the news media and are educating themselves - and educating others - outside the prison yard of broadcasting's tyranny.

Unlocking human potential

There was once a time when only a handful of people - the 'High Priests' - could read and write.
Everyone else had to shut up and do what they were told.

At the end of the Middle Ages, mechanical printing broke this monopoly. The change didn't occur over night, but from the time of the first western printing press literacy in advanced countries grew from less than 1% to well over 95%.

But one very important piece of the puzzle was missing...the ability of people to share their knowledge and experience with each other through publishing.

The pre-Internet publishing world, though far more

diverse than broadcasting, was still primarily a top-down, 'I-talk-you-listen' medium. The Internet shatters this paradigm and here's why this is so important:

As my old friend Ron Gross has written about frequently over the last thirty-plus years, the biggest advances in humanity have NOT come from 'The High Priests.' Progress comes from <u>individuals</u> of talent and determination who have the fortitude to go against 'business as usual' and bring something new, unique and valuable to the world.

This principle of progress applies to <u>all</u> fields of human endeavor - science, business, medicine, technology, the arts, you name it.

So, will the Internet save the world? No, not by itself. But it <u>has</u> created a near-miraculous platform for helping new ideas, and better ways of doing things find form and circulate much, much faster.

And that's the business I'm in. And you are too. <u>Keep up the good work!</u>

All Big Things Start Out Small

I used to wonder how Boeing, one of the world's largest airplane manufacturers ended up in the Seattle area. It sure can't be the sunny weather.

The other day I found out the story and it's instructive.

The founder of Boeing, William E. Boeing, started out in the timber industry. He got involved in flying purely as a hobby, seeing his first plane in 1909 at the Alaska-Yukon-Pacific Exhibition. A few years later he started taking flying lessons at a school operated by Glenn Martin, a car dealer from Southern California, who was one of the first airplane manufacturers.

Boeing became obsessed with aviation and decided he could build a better plane than the ones that were available at the time. Interestingly, his experience with wood came in handy because the original planes had many wooden parts. In 1916, he started his own aircraft manufacturing company. Then along came WWI, the US Navy had an urgent need for planes, and the rest is history...

One of the largest, most important manufacturing companies of all time started out... as someone's hobby.

Ten years ago this week

Ten years ago, Bill Gates, Larry Ellison, and even Steve Jobs were all on record as saying the Internet was a 'flash in the pan' and a diversion that would not amount to anything. (Their PR departments have since rewritten history, but you can look it up. They were all anti-Internet in the early 1990s.)

The big debate in the high tech world about the Internet was whether or not it could <u>ever</u> be successfully commercialized. Sentiment was split 50/50 among those who cared and most career Silicon Valley folks, including the leaders of the then 'cutting edge' multimedia industry who were not at all interested in the Internet's commercial potential.

Then, in the fall of 1994, a tremendous amount of 'behind the scenes' work suddenly began to bear fruit.

• On October 13, Mosaic (Netscape) released its first commercial browser...

• On October 27, HotWired, the first serious advertising-supported web site launched...

• On November 4, my company E-Media presented the world's first conference on the subject of advertising on the web featuring Marc Andreessen, the co-founder of Netscape. (Rick Boyce, one of my original online marketing students and one of the co-founders of Hot-Wired, was so tired from his launch that he slept in that day.)

All big things start out small

There was a time when all the people in the world who were passionate about making the Internet into a commercial medium could easily fit around a small table - and it wasn't that long ago.

None of us had any idea of where our fascination with the Internet would take us and believe me, for a long time, business-minded Internet people were considered the village idiots of Silicon Valley.

Don't be discouraged to start small. All big things start out that way. Let your enthusiasms guide you.

Thank Goodness

"Early to bed, early to rise, makes a man healthy, wealthy and wise." My hero, Benjamin Franklin said that, but he could have easily been talking about another practice... gratitude.

I don't know who originally cooked up the American holiday of 'Thanksgiving' but it is a spectacularly good idea. A day set aside to give thanks. Brilliant.

Gratitude seems to be a favorite subject of the wise. Buddha called it 'an attribute of noble persons.' In the Christian world 'Eucharist' is the Greek word for giving thanks.

Even non-religious savants like the Roman statesman Cicero and the German philosopher Friedrich Nietzsche had good things to say about gratitude. Cicero called it 'the parent of all other virtues' and Nietzsche called it 'the essence of all beautiful art.'

Discover the <u>scientific</u> way to become healthier, smarter and more energetic

Science - in the form of research data gathered by Robert A. Simmons, a professor of psychology at the University of California, Davis - recently demonstrated that the regular practice of thankfulness has a definite and positive transformative effect on people's lives.

Here's the experiment Simmons conducted. He took two groups of people: a control group that did nothing and a second group who spent a few minutes once a week jotting down who they should thank and for what.

Here's what Simmons found: In comparison with the control group, the group that kept a weekly 'thank you' journal "exercised regularly, reported fewer physical symptoms, felt better about their lives as a whole and were more optimistic about the upcoming week."

In a second experiment, he introduced something called a 'daily gratitude intervention' in which the test group spent a little time <u>every</u> <u>day</u> on focused gratitude. This group demonstrated "higher reported levels of alertness, enthusiasm, determination, attentiveness and energy." Makes sense. Gratitude is the reliving of positive memories and a workout of positive emotions. That's got to be good for your brain chemistry.

A modest proposal

As the year draws to a close, many businesses draw up an annual report tracing their accomplishments over the past year and their plans for the coming year. It's a great practice and well worth the time invested.

How about creating an annual report written from the point of view of gratitude? Making a detailed listing of all the things that went <u>right</u> this year? All the interesting new people you met, the relationships you strengthened, the breakthroughs in understanding you had. And when you're making your list of people and

198

things to be thankful for, don't forget a very important person... <u>you</u>.

In my experience, we're all pretty good at being hard on ourselves. So this year, after you've thanked all the people who've made you life richer this year, take a look at your own efforts - your diligence, your courage, your kindness - and remember to pat yourself on the back a bit too.

Thank you for being part of one of the most inspiring and satisfying years of my life and remember...

Your best is yet to come.

Lessons From a Gambler

I'm not particularly crazy about the gambling business, but it does offer everyone some interesting lessons on life and making a buck.

Here are some interesting tidbits I extracted from the autobiography of a famous gambler named 'Amarillo Slim.'

Each one merits an hour's meditation.

"Guessers always lose" - and other bits of wisdom from the gambling world

1. Guessers always lose

2. <u>Decisions</u> not results - Do the right thing enough times and the <u>results</u> will take care of themselves in the long run.

3. Choose the right opponents.

4. The guy who invented gambling was smart. The guy who invented chips was a <u>genius</u>.

5. Play the player more than you play the cards.

6. All you can do is make the plays that have a percentage of success and put yourself in a position to win.

7. It's a simple fact that the <u>less</u> you brag on something, the <u>more</u> it will sell.

8. Be tight <u>and</u> aggressive. Don't play many hands, but when you do play, be prepared to move in big.

9. Be able to quit a loser, and for goodness sakes, keep playing when you're winning.

10. Conduct yourself honorably so you're always invited back.

Business is not gambling, but sometimes it is a gamble

Someone once told me that one of the favorite pastimes of billionaires is playing poker. I don't know if that's true, but there certainly are a lot of lessons that translates very well from the poker table to business.

In business, you are always dealing with finite re-sources, uncertain outcomes, and players with their own agenda.

Some people sit down at the table and walk away with a big pile of chips. Other people leave their chips on the table. What makes the difference?

Focus, discipline, realism, having a plan, knowing and working the percentages - and being the kind of person who gets invited back. Sound simple? It is.

In Praise of Fathers

I got the news that my father had passed away when the phone rang at 1:30 AM in the morning.

We all knew it was coming. In fact, I'd been making arrangements to get a place in St. Augustine, FL, where he and my mother retired after a lifetime in the northeast, so I could spend more time with him. But the news was still a shock. I had just seen him a week before.

The timing was a bit rough. I had carved out a week to finish the sales letter for a big System Seminar that was coming up in just two months. (The Cleveland one.)

That planned week got telescoped down to the hours between 1:30 AM when I got the call and 7:30 AM when I got in the car and drove the 115 miles to Newark Airport to catch a flight to Florida.

When I left, the letter was 92% done, close enough for me to be able to steal a minute here and there to finish it when I got to Florida.

First Lesson from my Dad: When people are counting on you, get the job done. No excuses.

A different world

Some entrepreneurs come from entrepreneurial families. My Dad, God bless him, didn't have an entrepreneurial bone in his body.

He grew up on the wrong side of the Depression.

His family was part of the 25% of the country that didn't have a steady breadwinner in an era before safety nets. So his financial goal was not riches or business success, it was getting a good job he could not be arbitrarily fired from.

Though he and his brothers were bright, hard working young men, college was out of the question for them - but then World War II came along.

At an early point in his Army career, his sergeant announced that all the enlistees in his unit would be taking an aptitude exam.

A rumor spread that scoring high on the exam meant being assigned to a tough project and a lot of hard work, so 'the group' agreed to deliberately blow it. My Dad bucked the consensus. He decided to give the test his best shot and let the chips fall where they may.

He scored sky high on the exam and was chosen to receive training as an engineer, something the military was in desperate need of at the time. As a result, after his basic training, he spent a good part of the war in college. His colleagues were sent right into combat.

Second Lesson from my Dad: Be your best. Don't dumb yourself down to fit in with 'the group.'

Present at the creation

After the war, like so many other GIs, my Dad got the opportunity to go to college and get a degree.

With his family (his Mom, Dad and younger siblings) counting on him, he didn't screw around. He finished his BA in a year and a half, taking a double load of courses each semester and taking classes through the summer.

The goal was to get a paycheck as soon as possible so like a lot of new college grads, he took the first job offered to him. He became an auditor for a company that manufactured film and dyes.

Somewhere along the way, he discovered computers and I'm embarrassed to say that I don't know the details, but by the mid-1950s, before I was born, he entered what at the time was one of the rarest of professions: computing.

I remember visiting the places he worked as a kid. Computers in those days were roughly the size of refrigerators. Through a glass window on the top half of the box, you could see two large reels with tape, like a big tape recorder, going back and forth sort of like a washing machine.

This was the era before disc drives and random access memory. It was also the era before cathode ray tubes (CRTSs), also known as computer screens. If you wanted to know the contents of a computer, you had to print it out and read it on paper.

If you wanted to get a computer to do something, you had to write very specific, detailed instructions, one instruction per card and feed the cards into a machine. If you made one mistake, the process wouldn't work and then you had to print out the entire program and read it line by line to see where you'd gone wrong and try again.

My Dad's specialty was building and managing computer systems for big companies.

At various times, he was the top computer man at Knights of Columbus Insurance, Mattel Toys (great fun for us kids), Blue Cross/Blue Shield California and finally Blue Cross/Blue Shield New Jersey where he had 300 employees working under him and huge rooms filled with computers.

How did he do it? How did he make the transition from a struggling blue collar family to one of the top MIS (management information services) people in the insurance industry?

That's easy. He worked his butt off.

Third Lesson from my Dad: Hard work moves mountains.

You grow by helping others grow

My father's father intended to be a professional military man, but World War I changed his mind about that. When it was over, he decided he'd seen enough carnage to last a lifetime and entered civilian life.

When he was in the Army, he got involved in breaking the 'color barrier' by setting up a program to teach African American recruits from the South how to read. In those days, the gap between educational opportunities available to whites and African Americans, especially those from the South, was enormous.

Slavery had only been abolished just 50 years earlier and lynchings and terrorist organizations like the Klu Klux Klan were in full flower. Racism in the military at that time was still rampant and institutionalized.

My grandfather's reading program did not make him popular among some of his more 'tradition-minded' colleagues, but he didn't care. As the grandson of a man who fled religious and economic persecution in Ireland only to arrive in a city where storekeepers posted 'No dogs or Irish' on their windows, he wasn't going to be part of a system that kept other people down.

My father carried on this spirit in his own career. Because data processing was a brand new field, the ability to recruit, train and develop large numbers of new people was essential to every corporate MIS department's success. Because of the sheer size of the operations he managed, my father was responsible for launching a couple of thousand new people into the industry over the course of his career

He had the same attitude his father had which was that talent, character and hard work should be the only determining factor of a person's advancement. As a result, the MIS Department of Cross/Blue Shield New Jersey had a higher percentage of African American professionals than any other business organization of similar size in Newark, a city which in the late 60s and 70s was almost torn apart by racial polarization - literally.

Many of the people who were brought into the profession by my Dad went on to take positions in better paying industries (working for a state-regulated health insurance companies is no way to get rich.) It was frustrating to him to lose so many good people, but he was always glad to hear about one of 'his guys' going out and kicking ass in another industry.

Fourth Lesson from my Dad: Nothing beats the satisfaction of helping other people find their way and succeed.

Real World 101

My Dad bought computer equipment by the roomful in an era when everything related to computers was super-expensive. He was responsible for spending millions of dollars per year on everything related to running a 300 person corporate MIS department.

To give you an idea of the scope of his budget, when he ran Blue Cross/Blue Shield New Jersey's MIS Department, he was among the top 10% of IBM's commercial customers worldwide.

Though IBM wasn't in the bribery business (they didn't need to be) many of the smaller suppliers were.

In those days (and I'm sure it's still true), it was quite possible at the level my father was at to get rich from 'side deals' with various vendors. Payoffs came in the form of everything from cases of liquor to all expense paid vacations to the old stand by, cash in a paper bag.

My Dad had a simple policy. He'd only accept a 'gift' that he could keep on his desk at work in plan view. Everything else was sent back.

At Christmas time, returning the 'gifts' that vendors showered on him was a full time job for one of his staff members. They came in fast and furious.

As a kid, I couldn't fathom why my father would turn down all this 'free' stuff. I thought he was dumb.

Now I get it.

The world is full of people who'd like to buy your integrity for a handful of trinkets. Once you start down that slippery slope, it's all but impossible to turn back.

Fifth Lesson from my Dad: Play it straight. Be your own man and be worthy of the trust other people have placed in you.

Irony of ironies

There were two things I was sure about when I was growing up: 1) I would stay as far away from computers as possible (too boring) and 2) I would never work as hard as my Dad did (too dumb.)

After my father passed away, I was going through his papers and found the photo in this letter. (It's from 1957, almost fifty years ago.) I had never seen it before.

In fact, other than visiting him at work once in a blue moon, I really hadn't given any thought to his work or career.

I've since learned that my father was a pioneer in the field of Systems Analysis. Systems Analysis is taking complex activities and breaking them down into clear, easy-to-follow steps

So years after I decided not to go into computers and not to work as hard as my Dad, I find myself spending nearly every waking hour researching, studying and thinking about systems for making marketing and business management better.

I even named one of my companies, a seminar and training business, The System.

I wish my Dad could have seen all this come to pass, but I bet where ever he is, he's looking down having a good laugh.

If your Dad is still living, don't wait until he's gone to think about his accomplishments.

If he's passed, it's not too late to study his life and see what there is to learn from him.

And if you've got kids, don't be fooled. It may not look it, but they're watching you and absorbing every lesson, good and bad. My Dad wasn't perfect, no one is, but he sure left me with a fantastic legacy in the way he chose to live his life.

Happy Father's Day to all fathers, sons and daughters.

It's Called <u>Independence</u> Day
For a Reason

I'm not sure how Independence Day morphed into the Fourth of July - but I can make a good guess.

Independence Day <u>means</u> something. The Fourth of July is just a date on the calendar. It's kind of like calling Christmas 'The Twenty-fifth of July' or New Year's 'The First of January.' Dumb.

One of the features of a typical Independence Day celebration used to be a public reading - word for word - of the Declaration of Independence. They actually still do this in several towns in the region where I live, the Hudson River Valley, which was a major center of the conflict. Think Saratoga, West Point. Fort Ticonderoga. Washington slept here. A lot.

Everyone pretty much knows the "life, liberty and the pursuit of happiness" part of the Declaration of Independence. The opening phrase resonates in many people's memories too. "When in the course of human events...."

But how much of the Declaration of Independence do you actually know?

Why we fought

Here is a list of some of the things that Jefferson, Franklin, Washington and others found so objectionable about King George III's conduct that they were willing to risk 'life, liberty and limb' to oppose him:

• "He has refused his Assent to Laws, the most wholesome and necessary for the public.

• For imposing Taxes on us without our Consent.

• He is at this time transporting large Armies of foreign Mercenaries to complete the works of death, desolation and tyranny, already begun with circumstances of Cruelty and perfidy scarcely paralleled in the most barbarous ages, and totally unworthy the Head of a civilized nation. "

I have a theory as to why annual public readings of the Declaration of Independence have fallen out of favor and why Independence Day is now called 'The Fourth of July.'

• Reason #1: Independence is no longer a treasured virtue in our country.

• Reason #2: Many of the things that the Founding Fathers found so objectionable - like taxation without representation for example - have become institutionalized in the US.

Big business, big media, big government - the country seems to be run for their benefit today, not ours.

For example, just last week, the Supreme Court voted to uphold the right of New London, Connecticut to command a group of home owners to surrender their homes for the benefit of a privately owned corporation. My mind reels. A similar thing <u>almost </u>happened in my neck of the woods recently.

When the Declaration of Independence was written, 90% of Americans worked - and thought - for themselves. Today only 10% do. Of the 90% who work for a paycheck, over 55% work for institutions with 500 employees or more. That means nearly half of our country is financially beholden to some kind of big bureaucracy. Not a good thing.

One of the best things you can do for your country is to become economically independent - and use your economic independence to take a stand against the forces that routinely undermine our communities and our country. If people like us don't do it, who's going to?

Here : <u>www.TheSystemSeminar.com/hudson.gif</u> you'll find an article about a project I was part of which involved keeping a corporate bully from undermining the health and wealth of the region where I live. You can do stuff like this too.

<u>Happy Independence Day!</u>

Such a Deal

Here's the deal:

You've got to swim 2.4 miles. Then you've got to ride your bike 112 miles. Then you've got to run a marathon, 26.2 miles - all in one day.

And you've got to keep the pace up. If at any leg of the journey, you don't finish in time, you're out.

I can't guarantee the weather. It might be 100 degrees with 90% humidity. Or it could be pouring rain with golf ball sized hail bouncing off your skull.

That will be $500 please - non-refundable.

Oh, and you have 24 hours to get your registration in. The phone lines and web server get busy so it might take you an hour or so to get through.

Good luck.

Welcome to Iron Man USA

Somewhere in the distant recesses of my brain I once heard there was a thing called the Iron Man race, but it seemed too crazy to pay attention to. Sort of in the category of people who eat live goldfish or lie on beds of nails.

But the joke's on me.

Two weekends ago, 2000 people pounded the doors for the privilege to pay $500 to undergo deprivations that would violate every article of the Geneva Convention and make Attila the Hun wince at the harshness of it all.

And these folks do it voluntarily. They spend years and many thousands of dollars to prepare. And it's a high point in their lives.

Not only that, but their numbers are growing. New people are joining the sport all the time and from the first Iron Man held 27 years ago in Hawaii on a lark (only 12 people showed up), competitions are now held in practically every state in the Union and every reasonably developed country on earth.

Wait a minute... I thought people were becoming sloths, welded to their Lazy Boys with their TV remote controls fused to their hands.

Well, clearly many are, but some are going the opposite way. They're looking for a challenge with a capital 'C,' something that takes them out of the bleating herd and puts them on the bleeding edge of existence.

How can you use this?

Do you have an option in your product line that's INSANE? Something that demands a crazy level of commitment on the part of your customer. Something whose total cost is so exorbitant it takes even _your_ breath away...

And most important, something that gives your customers the chance to experience something so extreme that it blows past anything else in their lives.

It makes for an interesting mental exercise. Remember: Not every customer is on a budget. Not every customer has 'time considerations.' Not every customer wants to be coddled. And the 99% who do? They'll sit back in awe and buy the t-shirt and the hot dogs. It's a no-lose proposition.

Subtle and Deadly

It's that time of year again.

Ghosts, goblins and ghouls roam the streets. Witches and warlocks hold court. And the most frightening force on earth – kids binging on massive quantities of sugar – ravage homes across land.

But this week's letter is about something truly scary. Salesmanship.

A true story

The names have been changed to protect the guilty... actually, no one is guilty here, but this is a cautionary tale.

A good friend of mine, we'll call him Bob, introduced me to his good friend, we'll call him Tom.

I totally trust Bob's judgment and, as the old saying goes, any friend of Bob's is a friend of mine, so Tom was "in."

Tom was not trying to sell me anything. He was just sharing some info with me that he was passionate about and I was very interested in. We spent a very cordial hour on the phone. So far so good.

Then the monster reared its ugly head. Tom suddenly turned into a... a... a... salesman!

Arghhh!!!!

What happened?

Now, being a salesman myself, I have a lot of re-spect for salespeople. I'm even scrupulously polite to telemarketers and always wish them 'good luck' after I inform them that I'm not available to receive their call.

Here's the weird thing: Tom wasn't trying to sell me anything, but he did want me to do something and like Doctor Jekyll and Mr. Hyde, he suddenly shifted from a guy I was having an interesting conversation with into someone who was 'working' me.

Not because he asked me for something, but be-cause he suddenly started to talk like a salesman instead of a normal person. It was subtle – and deadly – and in an instant I forgot that we'd just spent a pleasant hour chatting on his dime and found myself mentally heading for the exit.

Subtle, but deadly.

When you read the copy of all the great salesmen from Claude Hopkins to David Ogilvy to Gary Bencivenga, you'll quickly be struck by the fact that their ad copy doesn't sound like ad copy. It sounds like an informed person sharing some fascinating, worth-while information with you.

Why do they write that way instead of using all the famous sales choke holds and closes?

It's simple and it's a perfect lesson for Halloween: People who look and act and sound like salesmen scare people.

By all means, be a salesman, just don't act like everyone's picture of one.

A Modest Proposal to Improve Thanksgiving

Thanksgiving is, hands down, my favorite holiday.

It doesn't compel frantic gift giving (like the commercialized version of Christmas), it doesn't promote excessive alcohol consumption and forced gaiety (like New Year's Day). In fact Thanksgiving is so laid back, it doesn't even require that folks exchange cards.

Instead, Thanksgiving celebrates the basics: food, family, and friends and the deep fun that accompanies taking the time to enjoy life's simple pleasures.

As icing on the cake, Thanksgiving encourages us - in its characteristically quiet and understated way - to take note of the things in our lives that are positive.

Gratitude is power

It's easy for entrepreneurs to fall into the trap of feeling that life is a never-ending struggle, where letting your guard down for a moment can mean ruin and every day is another day that the ever-growing "Must Do" list fails to get done.

If you don't know what I'm talking about, you are a very fortunate person indeed, but I have a feeling you may know a little about the outlook I'm describing.

How do we get ourselves out of this particular 'no win' trap?

Thanksgiving is the answer. Robert Emmons, a professor at the University of California, Davis, demonstrated through an elegant set of experiments not long ago that if you want to sleep better, feel better, and motivate yourself to take better care of your health, regular 'thanksgiving' sessions work magic.

Once a month...once a week...once a day

Right now we celebrate Thanksgiving once a year and, truth be told, it can be somewhat of a 'production' and actually be a bit stressful for some people.

But what if we had a Thanksgiving Day once a month? And what if we defined "Thanksgiving Day" to mean spending a whole day with the people you really want to be with just living: eating, talking, playing, resting, and being militantly free from worries (and ambitions) of any kind.

One day per month. Is there anyone so busy that they can't arrange at least one day per month for Thanksgiving?

Notice, by the way, that I said "arrange" not "find the time for." In my experience, trying to "find the time" rarely works. In contrast, arranging life to <u>make</u> the time for things has a nearly 100% success rate.

If it's a good idea to have Thanksgiving once a month, why not have it once a week? I'm talking about consistently carving out one day each week where you avoid the "busyness" of life and sit back to enjoy a good meal and revel in the pleasure of spending time with

226

people you love the most. That's what weekends used to be for. Remember?

Finally, if Thanksgiving makes sense once a week, why not once a day? A good meal, good company, peace and quiet, and attention not on the things that aren't working, that need to be improved, that are still undone, but dedicated to enjoying and appreciating the many things good in our lives.

Happy Thanksgiving Day!

A Class Act Worth Studying

Boardroom, Inc. (also known as Bottom Line Reports) is often cited as one of the greatest success stories in direct marketing history.

In fact, Marty Edelston was recently inducted into the Direct Marketers Hall of Fame.

He started where so many would be entrepreneurs start: long on ideas and short on money.

And he managed to leverage those two assets into a publishing company that has generated billions (yes billions) of dollars in direct sales by delivering high quality information about business, health, personal finances, and smart living to millions of subscribers and book buyers.

What's Marty's secret?

Hard work and dedication, of course.

A curious mind, endlessly open to new possibilities helped too.

Marty is also a genius at finding and surrounding himself with other great minds. He's made a science of it.

But I think his greatest secret can be summed up in three words:

"Life is long…"

Life is <u>long</u>?!

Many of us focus on how short life is and how little time there is to accomplish the things we want to get done.

But Marty takes a different view and now I am quoting directly from Hallie Mummert, the Editor and Chief of Target Marketing Magazine, who reported on this intriguing aspect of Marty's philosophy:

"1. Life is long…so strike business deals where everyone makes a reasonable – if not healthy – profit.

2. Life is long…so treat your vendors like partners, not your hired help. "It costs so little," Brian Kurtz said, "and it's great being everyone's favorite client."

3. Life is long…so treat all employees – past, present, and future – like family. Give them your best, and they will give you their best."

More than lip service

I can practically guarantee that you've heard a variation of these ideas before, but don't confuse them for platitudes.

Marty and the singular community he's formed over the last three decades live these principles. I can say that as someone who's had the pleasure of interacting with them on and off now for over ten years.

There's a lot of craft and technical know-how in our business, the business of Internet marketing, and there's also a lot of polished talk about 'win-win' and 'reciprocation', which sounds great from a podium.

Then there's reality: Life really is long and the greatest rewards go to those who actually 'get' this simple fact.

About Ken McCarthy

Ken McCarthy was one of the original pioneers of the movement to commercialize the Internet.

He sponsored the first conference on the subject of the Web's commercial potential in 1994 with the co-founder of Netscape Marc Andreessen.

That same year Ken wrote the first article on e-mail advertising that was published in a legitimate marketing industry trade journal. Rick Boyce, who is widely credited with popularizing the banner ad, credits Ken with introducing him to the idea that the Internet could be used as an advertising medium.

Ken's book "The Internet Business Manual" was the first book on Internet entrepreneurship published in Japan and for many years he served as a consultant to NEC, the Japanese equivalent to IBM, advising them on Internet matters.

Since 1993, Ken has developed numerous cutting edge training programs that have not only helped his clients make more money, but have also served to advance the state-of-the-art in Internet marketing practice.

Ken's System Seminar is now recognized as the foremost Internet marketing training in the world. Recently, the United States Patent and Trademark Office granted him the exclusive right to use the phrase "The System" to describe Internet marketing education products.

Before entering the Internet field, Ken produced concerts and radio programs; taught advanced learning strategies at MIT and Columbia University; worked on Wall Street; founded a direct marketing consulting company; and helped start an audio post production studio in New York City that was involved in the making of an Academy Award winning film and one of the highest grossing foreign language films of all time.

Ken's work both on and off the Internet has been acknowledged in a number of books including The Complete Guide to Internet Publicity by Steve O'Keefe, Peak Learning by Ron Gross, and How to Make Millions with Your Ideas by Dan Kennedy.

RESOURCES

To find out more about Ken and to visit his blogs
http://www.KenMcCarthy.com

Join the System Club

Join **The System Club** for a 30 day free trial membership. To learn more about this offer go here:
http://www.TheSystemClub.com/testdrive

System Home Study Courses:

System Smart Beginners – The foundations course for people who are new to Internet marketing and want to get the benefits of a System training without the expense of attending the live seminar:
http://www.SmartBeginners.com

Advanced Copywriting and Info Marketing Strategies – Learn exactly what it takes to build a six and seven figure a year information marketing business by someone who's done it and helped many others do it too.
http://www.KensCopyClinic.com

The System®
PO Box 42
Tivoli, NY 12583
845-757-5037
info@TheSystemSeminar.com